It's All About Relationships

What ITIL® doesn't tell you

It's All About Relationships

What ITIL® doesn't tell you

S. D. Van Hove, Ed.D.
Kathy S. Mills, MA/OD

IT Governance Publishing

Every possible effort has been made to ensure that the information contained in this book is accurate at the time of going to press, and the publisher and the author cannot accept responsibility for any errors or omissions, however caused. Any opinions expressed in this book are those of the author, not the publisher. Websites identified are for reference only, not endorsement, and any website visits are always at the reader's own risk. No responsibility for loss or damage occasioned to any person acting, or refraining from action, as a result of the material in this publication can be accepted by the publisher or the author.

Apart from any fair dealing for the purposes of research or private study, or criticism or review, as permitted under the Copyright, Designs and Patents Act 1988, this publication may only be reproduced, stored or transmitted, in any form, or by any means, with the prior permission in writing of the publisher or, in the case of reprographic reproduction, in accordance with the terms of licences issued by the Copyright Licensing Agency. Enquiries concerning reproduction outside those terms should be sent to the publisher at the following address:

IT Governance Publishing
IT Governance Limited
Unit 3, Clive Court
Bartholomew's Walk
Cambridgeshire Business Park
Ely
Cambridgeshire
CB7 4EA
United Kingdom

www.itgovernance.co.uk

First published in the United Kingdom in 2013
by IT Governance Publishing.

ISBN 978-1-84928-484-4

Foreword

I have been in the ITSM business as a consultant and instructor for more than 20 years, having achieved Service Manager when it was still ITIL®[1] V1. In my consulting and teaching practice, I could have used this book many, many times.

I have known one of the authors, Dr Suzanne Van Hove for many years and hold her in the highest regard. She is truly an expert in ITSM, not just by certificate but by her knowledge and uncanny sense of how Service Management works. Kathy's reputation speaks for itself. She too has considerable experience in this field and is well-equipped to be part of producing this book.

I graciously provide this foreword for their book.

ITIL is a framework and, as such, lacks the real depth of detail that practitioners often find themselves needing. In our journey to accomplish improvements and achieve the benefits of IT Service Management, we find that we need checklists, guides, process models, and more. If we do not have them, or cannot find them, we set to creating our own and realize there is a great deal of detail about the ITIL lifecycle phases and processes that we do not know.

In version 2 of ITIL, in the Service Manager programs we ran back then, a lot of time was spent with students helping them learn, memorize and internalize the interfaces between processes; the inputs and outputs, the glue that holds it all together. Well, there were only ten processes in that program so it was manageable for candidates to learn and memorize for their Service Manager exams.

ITIL today is considerably more complex (by virtue of being more complete and comprehensive). We also do not have the same exam requirements as before, so, for these two reasons, we no longer can or need to memorize all the relationship details. Still, we need this information and pouring through the ITIL core volumes, making our own lists is one way to approach it, if we have a lot of time on our hands.

Suzanne and Kathy saw that many ITSM practitioners and consultants have a need for one "list" and set about creating this book which documents the inputs and outputs, process to process, phase to phase. Their tables are easy to read and follow, and the whole book is well organized. Functions are covered as well, giving you everything you need; whether for study, personal interest, or an ITSM project. Just assigned as a process manager? This book is for you, to understand what you need and can expect from other functions and processes and what you will need to provide in return.

I cannot imagine trying to create process documentation or working on a process project without this valuable text. Well, actually, I guess I can because I have had to do it! I wish I had this book long ago.

Suzanne's and Kathy's knowledge and attention to detail shine through in the very high quality of this publication. No doubt you will find it indispensable and in short order, I'm sure your copy will be well used and dog-eared.

Dwight Kayto PMP, ITSM Fellow, ITIL Expert - March 2013.

---

[1] ITIL® is a registered trade mark of the Cabinet Office

Preface

When we embarked on writing this information, we came at it with the perspective of giving the Service Manager a view into how all the processes and functions work together. For anyone who has spent time reading the core volumes, the information is useful, but it takes valuable time to connect all the details to then determine what is relevant. We wanted to provide that view, making it easier for the process owners and managers to mature their processes.

We both recognize that, as you look through the lists, you may have some additional ideas of what should be included, as well as some elements you may think are not relevant. Our goal is not to list every possible connection, but to list as many as possible and hopefully assist you in thinking differently about the framework. If you find yourself identifying additional relationships, or seeing the processes as part of a larger relationship rather than a single process, then we have succeeded at what we set out to do.

Suzanne and Kathy

About the Authors

Dr Suzanne D. Van Hove, founder and CEO of SED-IT, is currently managing the consultancy and education programs of the 15-year-old Service Management-based company. Previous life experiences were focused in the educational profession – teaching at all levels, from kindergarten through post-doctoral programs. Working in the educational and sports industries has been a perfect segue to Service Management – it is all about performance! One would be hard pressed to find a professional vertical she has not touched. Dr Van Hove holds degrees from Boston University, Ithaca College, and DePauw University and certifications in ITIL and ISO/IEC 20000.

Dr Van Hove continues to be active in itSMF USA (Knowledge Management portfolio owner, 2009–2012) as well as within the international community. A frequent international speaker and co-writer of priSM® (Professional Recognition for IT Service Management), she is an advocate for professionalism within Service Management and the inclusion of Service Management in higher education programs. An opera aficionado and an avid rosebush gardener, Dr Van Hove currently resides in Louisville, KY.

Kathy S. Mills is currently working for a Fortune 100 company as the Service Planning Manager. With 18 years of experience working in IT, she has served in various customer and service oriented environments. Kathy has been responsible for building and implementing plans for taking the ITIL best practice and identifying a multi-year implementation plan. The combination of her experience, her Masters in Organizational Development (University of Phoenix), and her eight years of corporate training, provides the unique perspective of understanding the technical needs and the human factor of adapting change into the standards and outputs of the company.

Her experience ranges from consulting with the federal government and US military, as well as working in international non-profit and Fortune 100 companies. Kathy, along with her husband and two children have lived in San Diego, San Jose, Seattle, and the DC area. She enjoys playing the piano, hiking, watching good movies, and playing at Disneyland. Kathy and her family live in Northridge, CA.

Acknowledgements

The authors would like to thank Paul Mungall, for his encouragement and support in the value of this work.

We each want to thank all who have offered their personal support and encouragement over the years – you are too many to name individually but know, we know that we would not have accomplished what we have without you; our deepest thanks and gratitude to each of you.

We also would specifically like to thank the following reviewers for their helpful suggestions and keen eyes: Jay Stuart, Steve Matthews, Brian Johnson, CA, Dave Jones, Pink Elephant, and Chris Evans, ITSM specialist.

Contents

Introduction

As the ITIL framework matures and expands the definition of the processes and functions in a best practice organization, the process owners and managers, as well as the leadership, have to shift their discussions and perspectives. In early adopt and adapt initiatives, it was common practice to look at a single process and work towards the implementation and operationalization of that specific process. Typically, as the focus turned to the next process, the connection between the first process and the new one often was minimally defined or, even worse, the new process was designed to correct the "mistakes" of the preceding process. Slowly, our thinking has evolved.

However, with the complexity and number of processes in the current framework, as well as the challenge of implementing change without detrimentally affecting the operational environment, we may be perpetuating the mistakes of old. Today's discussions and plans for improvements are fast and furious, if only to keep up with business demands and technology changes. Enough time to truly understand and manage the relationships between the processes and functions is not typically available or planned. This is a risk that organizational leadership should dedicate serious thought to, and create an environment where the individual process, as well as the community of processes, are assessed, managed, and improved.

As companies mature in how they deploy the framework, they will quickly realize that, to truly achieve the value that is embedded in the framework, the relationships have to be managed and maintained in tandem with the processes. Just as change to the environment is controlled and managed, any change to the supporting processes has to include the same assessment rigor, specifically, what are the downstream and upstream impacts of process change. This "forest" view of the Service Management processes demands an understanding that process output will impact the next activity within the process but it may also impact other the related processes. In any case, this potential impact must be controlled and managed so that the risk of poor service, unachieved goals and objectives, resource waste, and the many other risks associated with Service Management do not arise.

This guide provides a view into those relationships, from clear work products and deliverables to less measurable outcomes which are still critical to the success of the processes. By seeing the processes in this fashion, all stakeholders can fully embrace the value of Service Management as described within the ITIL framework.

We would be remiss if we did not point out that there is a set of relationships which are not included. As we built these tables, gleaning information from the core ITIL volumes, from our practical experience, and from other frameworks, there were times, based on our practical experience, when an outcome (either a relationship or decision) did not "fit" in the ITIL-based processes. This is where the ISO/IEC 20000 family of standards enters. ISO/IEC 20000-1:2011 is all about the Service Management System (SMS) where we have a series of processes that govern and manage the familiar Service Management processes (e.g. Service Level Management, Business Relationship Management, Change Management, etc.).

The SMS is the tone, the environment governance that is defined and managed. Even though the ITIL framework stresses the strategic aspects of Service Management in ITIL Service Strategy (which does provide elements of governance), we are still missing the piece where we have unequivocally defined the elements of management responsibility, documentation management, and resource management, to name just a few ISO/IEC

20000 concepts. The most powerful requirement within ISO/IEC 20000 is the fact that top management is defined, documented, and its actions measured – especially its commitment to the Service Management initiative. So, as you look at these relationships, consider looking one layer higher within the SMS. Get a copy of the standard and consider how clearly defining your SMS will further mature your initiative.

How to Use this Information

For each process and function within the ITIL lifecycle, we have listed several points:

- How the process outputs are used by other processes and functions (gives)
  - Input from <named process> to …
- How the process uses outputs from other processes and functions (gets)
  - Output from … to <named process>

    The "…" is representing the process listed in the far left column of the tables and <named process> is the process being discussed.

Understand that the inputs and outputs from these processes and functions can include reports, data/information, and/or other specific documents.

Because this is an acronym-heavy framework (and professional vertical), we have listed the acronyms used within the tables in the Acronyms chart.

Lastly, we conclude with a master listing of "work products" – anything from specifically named reports and documents to some of the more innocuous outputs – from each process.

Acronyms

Processes and Functions (*italics*)

7S	7-step Improvement Process (CSI)
AcM	Access Management (SO)
AM	Availability Management (SD)
AppM	*Application Management (SO)*
BRM	Business Relationship Management (SS)
CapM	Capacity Management (SD)
ChE	Change Evaluation (ST)
ChM	Change Management (ST)
DC	Design Coordination (SD)
DM	Demand Management (SS)
EM	Event Management (SO)
FM	Financial Management for IT Services (SS)
IM	Incident Management (SO)
ISM	Information Security Management (SD)
ITOM	*IT Operations Management (SO)*
ITSCM	IT Service Continuity Management (SD)
KM	Knowledge Management (ST)
PM	Problem Management (SO)
RDM	Release and Deployment Management (ST)
RF	Request Fulfillment (SO)
SACM	Service Asset and Configuration Management (ST)
SCatM	Service Catalogue Management (SD)
	Service Desk (SO)
SLM	Service Level Management (SD)
SPM	Service Portfolio Management (SS)
StM	Strategy Management for IT Services (SS)
SuppM	Supplier Management (SD)
SVT	Service Validation and Testing (ST)
TM	*Technical Management (SO)*
TPS	Transition Planning and Support (ST)

Note: Service Desk will not be abbreviated owing to possible confusion with Service Design

Terms

AMIS	Availability Management Information System (AM)
AppDev	Application Development
BCM	Business Capacity Management (CapM)
BCP	Business Continuity Plan
BIA	Business Impact Analysis (ITSCM)
CAB	Change Advisory Board (ChM)
CAPEX	Capital Expense (FM)
CFIA	Component Failure Impact Analysis (AM)
CI	Configuration Item (SACM)
CIA	Confidentiality, Integrity, Availability (ISM)
CMDB	Configuration Management Database (SACM)
CMIS	Capacity Management Information System (CapM)
CMS	Configuration Management System (SACM)
CSF	Critical Success Factor (CSI)
CS	Change Schedule (ChM)
CSI	Continual Service Improvement
DIKW	Data-to-Information-to-Knowledge-to-Wisdom (KM)
DML	Definitive Media Library (SACM/RDM)
DR	Disaster Recovery (ITSCM)
ECAB	Emergency Change Advisory Board (ChM)
ELS	Early Life Support (RDM)
FTA	Fault Tolerance Analysis (AM)
ITIL	Information Technology Infrastructure Library
ITSM	IT Service Management
KE	Known Error (PM)
KEDB	Known Error Database (PM)
KPI	Key Performance Indicators (CSI)
MI	Management Information
OLA	Operational Level Agreement (SLM)
OPEX	Operational Expense (FM)
PBA	Patterns of Business Activity (DM)
PIR	Post-Implementation Review (ChM)
PMO	Project Management Office
PSO	Projected Service Outage (ChM, AM, SLM)

RFC	Request for Change (ChM)	RCA	Root Cause Analysis (PM)
ROI	Return on Investment (FM)	SLR	Service Level Requirement (SLM)
SAC	Service Acceptance Criteria (Appendix B, *ITIL Service Design*)	SM	Service Management
		SMIS	Security Management Information System
SCM	Service Capacity Management (CapM)	SO	Service Operation
SCMIS	Supplier and Contract Management Information System (SuppM)	SOA	Service Outage Analysis (AM)
		SPOF	Single Point of Failure (AM)
SD	Service Design	SQP	Service Quality Plan (SLM)
SDP	Service Design Package (DC)	SS	Service Strategy
SFA	Service Failure Analysis (AM)	ST	Service Transition
SIP	Service Improvement Plan (SLM)	TCO	Total Cost of Ownership (FM)
SKMS	Service Knowledge Management System (KM)	TCU	Total Cost Utilization (FM)
		TO	Technical Observation (AM)
SLA	Service Level Agreement (SLM)	UAT	User Acceptance Testing (RDM)
SLAM	Service Level Agreement Monitoring (SLM)	UC	Underpinning Contract (SuppM/SLM)
		UP	User Profiles (DM)
		VOI	Value of Investment (FM/CSI)

Service Strategy (SS)

Purpose

Define the strategic intentions of a Service Provider (what is important, define the plans, how to make decisions, etc.) in order to meet organizational outcomes.

Objectives

- Define and operationalize "strategy."
- From the view of the customer, define and operationalize "service."
- Understand value – its creation and delivery.
- Manage all aspects of service delivery – assets, funding, purpose, etc. – to the benefit of the customer and Service Provider.
- Define the relationships (service, IT, business, etc.) that perpetuate and grow in order to achieve the necessary business outcomes.

Lifecycle stage (…)	Input from SS to …	Output from … to SS
Service Design	<ul><li>Vision and mission</li><li>Service Portfolio</li><li>Policies</li><li>Strategies and strategic plans</li><li>Priorities</li><li>Service charters including service packages and details of utility and warranty</li><li>Financial information and budgets</li><li>Documented patterns of business activity (PBA) and user profiles (UPs)</li><li>Service models</li></ul>	<ul><li>Input to business cases and the Service Portfolio</li><li>Service Design Packages (SDPs)</li><li>Updated service models</li><li>Service Portfolio updates including the Service Catalogue</li><li>Financial estimates and reports</li><li>Design-related knowledge and information in the Service Knowledge Management System (SKMS)</li><li>Designs for Service Strategy processes and procedures</li></ul>
Service Transition	<ul><li>Vision and mission</li><li>Service Portfolio</li><li>Policies</li><li>Strategies and strategic plans</li><li>Priorities</li><li>Change proposals, including utility and warranty requirements and expected timescales</li><li>Financial information and budgets</li><li>Input to Change evaluation and Change Advisory Board (CAB) meetings</li></ul>	<ul><li>Transitioned Services</li><li>Information and feedback for business cases and Service Portfolio</li><li>Response to change proposals</li><li>Service Portfolio updates</li><li>Change schedule</li><li>Feedback on strategies and policies</li><li>Financial information for input to budgets</li><li>Financial reports</li><li>Knowledge and information in the SKMS</li></ul>

Lifecycle stage (...)	Input from SS to ...	Output from ... to SS
Service Operation	• Vision and mission • Service Portfolio • Policies • Strategies and strategic plans • Priorities • Financial information and budgets • Demand forecasts and strategies • Strategic risks	• Operating risks • Operating cost information for Total Cost of Ownership (TCO) calculations • Actual performance data
Continual Service Improvement	• Vision and mission • Service Portfolio • Policies • Strategies and strategic plans • Priorities • Financial information and budgets • PBA • Achievements against metrics, key performance indicators (KPIs) and critical success factors (CSFs) • Improvement opportunities logged in the Continual Service Improvement (CSI) register	• Results of customer and user satisfaction surveys • Input to business cases and the Service Portfolio • Feedback on strategies and policies • Financial information regarding improvement initiatives for input to budgets • Data required for metrics, KPIs, CSFs • Service reports • Requests for change (RFCs) for implementing improvements

From *ITIL® Service Strategy*, Table 3.21 ©Crown Copyright 2011. Reproduced under license from the Cabinet Office.

Strategy Management for IT Services (StM)

Purpose

Defines and maintains organizational strategic plans, policies, and perspectives as they relate to service delivery, including the management of those services which enable the achievement of business goals/objectives.

Objectives

- Understand the internal and external environment and identify opportunities to exploit for the benefit of the organization.
- Identify potential constraints to the achievement of business outcomes and define mitigation actions.
- Clearly define and manage the Service Provider's vision for ongoing relevance.
- Ensure services delivered meet the needs of its customers (current/future perspective).
- Define and manage current (up-to-date) appropriate planning documents.
- Ensure proper dissemination of the plans to tactical and operational plans.
- Ensure all strategic changes are properly reflected in documentation and are appropriate to changes in the internal and external environments.

Process (...)	Input from StM to ...	Output from ... to StM
Service Strategy		
Service Portfolio Management	<ul><li>Mission/vision</li><li>Service strategies and plans</li><li>Policies</li><li>Objectives, policies, and limits for the development of the Service Portfolio</li><li>Determination of type of service to include based on Strategy</li><li>Determines objectives for service investment</li><li>Determines ideal market space</li></ul>	<ul><li>Services in Pipeline/Service Catalogue</li><li>Strategic objective(s) fulfilled by Services</li><li>Service models</li><li>Strategic risks</li><li>Return on Investment (ROI) of Services in Service Portfolio</li></ul>
Financial Management	<ul><li>Mission/vision</li><li>Defines ROI necessary from service delivery</li><li>Defines investment parameters</li><li>Resources used in managing the StM process</li><li>Proposed process budget</li></ul>	<ul><li>Financial information to influence prioritization of actions/plans</li><li>Service investment analysis</li><li>Service valuation</li><li>ROI/Value of Investment (VOI) calculations</li><li>Cost of StM activities</li><li>Budget for strategic plans</li><li>Track/report on achievement of strategic objectives (financial view)</li></ul>
Demand Management	<ul><li>Mission/vision</li></ul>	<ul><li>PBA</li></ul>

Process (...)	Input from StM to ...	Output from ... to StM
Demand Management cont.	• Service strategies • Key business outcomes and business activities (for PBAs/UPs)	• UPs • Confirmation that current mitigation techniques are in line with Strategy
Business Relationship Management	• Mission/vision • Service strategies • Policies • Strategic plans, perspectives, policies • Business outcomes met by various Services	• Information about the customer (e.g. objectives, environment, requirements) • Defined business outcomes • Customer Portfolio • Validates changes of requirements, design, funding, design model or strategy to the Service Strategy
Service Design		
Design Coordination	• Mission/vision • Service Strategy • Defines policies that must be met when designing Services • Defines what design efforts require DC efforts • Defines constraints that must be addressed by designs • Defines specific outcomes Services need to achieve • Service charter • Service models • Governance policies • Legal, regulatory, statutory requirements	• Plans/designs that address (meet) the strategic objectives (SDP)
Service Catalogue Management	• Mission/vision • Service Strategy • Policies	• Up-to-date Service Catalogue
Service Level Management	• Mission/vision • Service Strategy • Policies • Strategy requirements for new/changed Services • Project Portfolio (owned by Project Management Office (PMO)) • Constraints	• Customer Agreement Portfolio • Service reports (achievement of strategic objectives) • Service Quality Plan (SQP) • Results of service reviews/improvements
Availability Management	• Mission/vision • Service Strategy • Policies • Strategy requirements for new/changed Services • Project Portfolio (owned by PMO)	• Availability Plan • Designs meeting strategic requirements • Links of Service Designs to business outcomes • Proactive Availability Management (AM) measures • Risk assessment and countermeasures

Process (...)	Input from StM to ...	Output from ... to StM
Capacity Management	• Mission/vision • Service Strategy • Policies • Strategy requirements for new/changed Services • Project Portfolio (owned by PMO)	• Capacity Plan • Proactive Capacity Management (CapM) measures • Business Capacity Management (BCM) and Service Capacity Management (SCM) activities supporting and enhancing organizational strategy
IT Service Continuity Management	• Mission/vision • Service Strategy • Policies • Business Strategy, plans, risk tolerance • Strategy requirements for new/changed Services • Project Portfolio (owned by PMO) • Provides definition of "disaster"	• IT Service Continuity (ITSCM) policy which meets mission/vision • ITSCM Plans/measures in place to meet Service Strategy • Risk assessment and countermeasures • Review of strategy/plans from a Continuity perspective
Information Security Management	• Mission/vision • Service Strategy • Policies • Strategy requirements for new/changed Services • Project Portfolio (owned by PMO) • Business Strategy policies/plans • Business plans (current/future) • Risks • Change to corporate governance • Business security policy • Corporate risk management • Review/revision of IT Strategy, plans, and policies	• Information Security Management (ISM) policy meeting mission/vision • Security controls to enhance achievement of the Service Strategy • Reports on security breaches
Supplier Management	• Mission/vision • Service Strategy • Policies • Strategy requirements for new/changed Services • New/changed corporate governance • New/changed IT governance	• Supplier/contract performance reports (to meet Strategy)

Process (...)	Input from StM to ...	Output from ... to StM
Service Transition		
Transition Planning and Support	<ul><li>Mission/vision</li><li>Service Strategy (underpins Transition policies)</li><li>Policies</li><li>Input to Service Transition protocols</li></ul>	<ul><li>Actions and plans for cultural, organizational and Service Changes to meet strategic plans</li><li>Transition policies</li></ul>
Change Management	<ul><li>Mission/vision</li><li>Service Strategy</li><li>Strategic plans</li><li>Policies</li><li>Defines Changes and the extent of Change (ensure change contributes to the achievement of the overall Strategy)</li><li>RFC for process improvements</li></ul>	<ul><li>Approved strategic plans, policies</li><li>Actions/plans for cultural, organizational and Service Changes to meet strategic plans</li></ul>
Service Asset and Configuration Management	<ul><li>Mission/vision</li><li>Service Strategy</li><li>Policies</li><li>Process artifacts recorded as CIs</li></ul>	<ul><li>Use/deployment of corporate assets/CIs</li></ul>
Release and Deployment Management	<ul><li>Mission/vision</li><li>Service Strategy</li><li>Policies</li><li>Application Portfolio (typically owned by AppDev)</li><li>Guidance for Release Policy development based on overall strategic view</li></ul>	<ul><li>Actions and plans for cultural, organizational and Service Changes to meet strategic plans</li><li>Service Transition (ST) Report</li><li>Release policies</li></ul>
Service Validation and Testing	<ul><li>Mission/vision</li><li>Service Strategy</li><li>Policies</li><li>Parameters for testing to ensure achievement of strategic objectives</li><li>Appropriate recognition, funding, resources, and communication around testing</li></ul>	<ul><li>Actions and plans for cultural, organizational, and Service Changes to meet strategic plans</li></ul>
Change Evaluation	<ul><li>Mission/vision</li><li>Service Strategy</li><li>Policies</li><li>Information to prioritize and evaluate Services ensuring they are built to original intent</li></ul>	<ul><li>Any agreed variation from original intent feed back into Strategy for adjustments and validation</li></ul>
Knowledge Management	<ul><li>Mission/vision</li><li>Service Strategy</li><li>Policies</li><li>Accurate capture, store, use, and manage process information and data (SKMS)</li></ul>	<ul><li>Structures information for use in strategic decisions (understand environment, history, dynamics, etc.)</li><li>Relevant, timely, required, and accurate knowledge, information and data</li></ul>

Process (...)	Input from StM to ...	Output from ... to StM
Service Operation		
Event Management	• Mission/vision • Service Strategy • Policies • Generic guidelines (scope) of operation (within defined Strategy)	• Management information (MI) measuring achievement (or not) of Strategy • Measurements from tools calibrated to indicate if Strategy is effective
Incident Management	• Mission/vision • Service Strategy • Policies • Generic guidelines (scope) of operation (within defined Strategy)	• Execution of strategic priorities • MI measuring achievement (or not) of Strategy
Request Fulfillment	• Mission/vision • Service Strategy • Policies • Generic guidelines (scope) of operation (within defined Strategy)	• MI measuring achievement (or not) of Strategy
Problem Management	• Mission/vision • Service Strategy • Policies • Generic guidelines (scope) of operation (within defined Strategy)	• MI measuring achievement (or not) of Strategy
Access Management	• Mission/vision • Service Strategy • Policies • Generic guidelines (scope) of operation (within defined Strategy)	• MI measuring achievement (or not) of Strategy
Continual Service Improvement		
7-step Improvement Process	• Mission/vision • Service Strategy • Policies • Strategic parameters • Service improvement opportunities • Specific service improvements based on StM events • Corporate, divisional, and departmental goals/objectives • Legislative/regulatory requirements • Governance requirements • Risk assessment • Identify improvement opportunities	• Measurements/reports as to the effective Strategy execution • Evaluate Strategy for effectiveness • Improvements to Strategy (process, service, etc.) • Gap analysis (as-is vs to-be; planned vs actual, etc) • Service improvement opportunities • Improvement possibilities for assessment against the Strategy • Recommendations for improvement implantation plans

Function (...)	Input from StM to ...	Output from ... to StM
Service Desk	• Mission/vision • Service Strategy	• Opportunities to consider (based on caller information/ suggestions) in Strategy review/improvement
Technical Management	• Mission/vision • Service Strategy	
Application Management	• Mission/vision • Service Strategy	
IT Operations Management	• Mission/vision • Service Strategy	

Service Portfolio Management (SPM)

Purpose

Ensures the Service Provider delivers the "right" services balancing IT investment with the action of meeting business needs; works with the other Service Management (SM) processes to ensure necessary returns are achieved; definitively links the service to the achievement of business outcome.

Objectives

- Provide the means to assess and confirm which Services to provide based on the necessary return and inherent risk.
- Keep a current Portfolio clearly indicating which Service meets what business need and business outcome.
- Provide a Service evaluation method that indicates whether or not the Strategy was met and takes into account internal and external environmental change.
- Control what Services are offered as well as the level and conditions.
- Track lifecycle service investment; this enables the evaluation of the defined Strategy and how well it has been met.
- Analyze Services for viability; retire those no longer meeting the need.

Process (...)	Input from SPM to ...	Output from ... to SPM
Service Strategy		
Strategy Management for IT Services	<ul><li>Services in Pipeline/Service Catalogue</li><li>Strategic objective(s) fulfilled by Services</li><li>Service models</li><li>Strategic risks</li><li>ROI of Services in Service Portfolio</li></ul>	<ul><li>Mission/vision statement</li><li>Service strategies and plans</li><li>Policies</li><li>Objectives, policies and limits for the development of the Service Portfolio</li><li>Determination of type of Service to include based on Strategy</li><li>Determines objectives for Service investment</li><li>Determines ideal market space</li></ul>
Financial Management	<ul><li>Service structure that defines cost model, accounting, and budgeting system; basis for charging</li><li>Service Portfolio</li><li>Customer Portfolio</li><li>Customer Agreement Portfolio</li><li>Project Portfolio</li><li>Application Portfolio</li><li>Resources used in managing the SPM process</li><li>Service packages</li><li>Market spaces</li><li>Service models</li></ul>	<ul><li>Cost of SPM activities</li><li>Budget approval</li><li>Tools/information to perform ROI calculations</li><li>Financial reports</li><li>Business case evaluation for new/changed Service (accept/reject decision)</li></ul>

Process (...)	Input from SPM to ...	Output from ... to SPM
Financial Management cont.	• Services in pipeline (under review/in development) • Services to be/are retired • Proposed process budget	
Demand Management	• Return of Services currently delivered (understand criticality and impact of Services to organization to manage demand) • Initiate a new/changed Service • Validation of Service models • Validation of Service packages Customer Portfolio • Service Portfolio • Customer Agreement Portfolio	• PBAs/UPs • Differentiated offerings for Service packages • Create/evaluate Service models • Establish/forecast utilization • Identify different types of users • Service package definition • Projected demand for Services/Service packages
Business Relationship Management	• Up-to-date Service Portfolio • Service models • Market spaces • Application Portfolio • Project Portfolio • Service charters • Service proposals • Status reports on new/changed Services • Business case evaluation for new/changed Service (accept/reject decision)	• Initiate Request for new/changed Services • Provides business information • Service requirements • Business requirements (objectives, outcomes, priorities) • Customer Portfolio • Customer Agreement Portfolio (SLM) • Suggestions or complaints • Business case evaluation for new/changed Service (accept/reject decision) • Market space suggestions • Business case for a new/changing Service
Service Design		
Design Coordination	• Service Portfolio • Service charter • Change proposal • Business case • Business requirements • Design work prioritized to business need • How the Service will be measured by the business • Linkage between Service component/asset and business outcome • Market space information • Utility/warranty requirements • Service options • Risks • Priorities • Project Portfolio (PMO)	• SDP • Service Portfolio updates • Updated Service models • Project updates

Process (...)	Input from SPM to ...	Output from ... to SPM
Service Catalogue Management	• Service charter • Change proposals • Determines which Services and Service packages to include in the Service Catalogue • Information to include in Service descriptions/Service Catalogue • Service packages	• Service definition • Service Portfolio updates (ensures Service Catalogue and Portfolio "agree") • Builds and maintains the Service Catalogue
Service Level Management	• Portfolio, Pipeline, Retired Services • Customer Portfolio • Customer Agreement Portfolio • Application Portfolio • Project Portfolio (PMO) • Service models • Market spaces • Strategic risks	• Manages Services to achieve agreed Service levels • Reports on achieved Service levels • Customer Agreement Portfolio • Service reports (achievement of business outcome)
Availability Management	• Availability targets • Reports on the status of new/changed Services • Business demands • Service Information	• Availability Plan (current investment and future availability needs) • AMIS
Capacity Management	• Reports on the status of new/changed Services • Business plans/requirements • Service Portfolio	• Capacity Plan (current investment and future capacity needs) • CMIS
IT Service Continuity Management	• Services that must be considered for Continuity planning, as agreed • Recovery criteria • Risk information • New/changed Services • Service Portfolio • Service Catalogue • Customer Portfolio • Customer Agreement Portfolio	• ITSCM Plan (current countermeasures and recovery plans for each Service) • Business Impact Analysis (BIA) (risks) • Capabilities for Continuity actions
Information Security Management	• Service Portfolio • New/changed Services • Service information • Strategic risks • Service models	• Security checks on access to Service Portfolio • Security controls • SMIS
Supplier Management	• New/changed Services • Service Portfolio • Project Portfolio (PMO) • Customer Portfolio • Customer Agreement Portfolio • Application Portfolio	• SCMIS • Supplier/contract performance report • At risk suppliers/contract • Links between Suppliers and Services provided (SCMIS/CMDB/CMS/SKMS)

Process (...)	Input from SPM to ...	Output from ... to SPM
Service Transition		
Transition Planning and Support	• Service Portfolio and supporting portfolios for a full picture of Service delivery and customers • Submission of change proposals	• Transition updates
Change Management	• Service charters • Service Portfolio • Service Package descriptions • Service models • Change proposals • Service charter • Strategic risks • RFCs for improvement (process activities, services, etc.)	• Authorizes change proposals and charters • Assesses resources to support change proposals and charters • Mitigates risk to Services as new/changed Service is designed, built, released
Service Asset and Configuration Management	• "Documents" managed via the CMDB/CMS	• CMS supports the Service Portfolio and all its components • Provides data/information for Service models • Relationships between CIs, Service assets and Service delivery
Release and Deployment Management	• Service Portfolio, Service Catalogue, retired Services	• New Service to Service Catalogue (SCatM)
Service Validation and Testing	• Strategic risks	• Confirmation of Service functionality based on testing activities • Confirmation of anticipated Service return
Change Evaluation	• Change proposal • Requirements/risks which are used to assess the new/changed Service	• Interim/final Evaluation reports (ChM)
Knowledge Management	• Service Portfolio (Service Pipeline, Service Catalogue, Retired Services) • Market space research • Risk research • Various portfolios • Accurate capture, store, use, and manage process information and data • Update of Service Portfolio	• Relevant, timely, required, and accurate knowledge, information, and data

Process (...)	Input from SPM to ...	Output from ... to SPM
Service Operation		
Event Management	• Overall view of Service (how and why delivered)	• Information for events related to a Service • Standard operating procedures • Escalation procedures • Prioritization
Incident Management	• Overall view of Service (how and why delivered)	• Service recommendations from incident patterns • Standard operating procedures • Escalation procedure • Prioritization
Request Fulfillment		• List of defined, documented and approved Service Requests
Problem Management	• Overall view of Service (how and why delivered)	• Standard operating procedures • Escalation procedures • Prioritization
Access Management	• User access/profile requirements • List of users/groups authorized to access the Service Portfolio	• Reports on requests for Service Portfolio access • Reports on unauthorized access attempts
Continual Service Improvement		
7-step Improvement Process	• Service Portfolio • Service models • Risk assessment • Market expectations (market space analysis) • Identify improvement opportunities	• Improvement possibilities for assessment against the current Service Portfolio • Business case evaluation • Validate Service objectives • Analysis of actual vs anticipated use and return of various Services (use to improve Services, make changes to the mix or availability of Services) • Recommendations for improvement implantation plans

Function (...)	Input from SPM to ...	Output from ... to SPM
Service Desk	• Various portfolios	• Information update request
Technical Management		• Support of underlying technology for process activities /work products • Research/develop solutions to expand the Service Portfolio
Application Management		• Application Portfolio • Support of underlying technology for process activities /work products
IT Operations Management		

Financial Management for IT Services (FM)

Purpose

Acquire necessary funds to design, develop, and deliver Services that meet the strategic needs of the organization.

Objectives

- Define the necessary processes and procedures to calculate, manage, and communicate Service costs.
- Evaluate the financial impact to the Service Provider of Strategy changes.
- Acquire funding to manage Service provision.
- Ensure good use of customer/Service assets to meet organizational objectives.
- Differentiate between income and expense; ensure they are balanced and in line with organizational financial policies.
- Manage/report Service provision expenditures to appropriate/agreed parties.
- Perform financial policies/practices as dictated.
- Define financial spend for the design, delivery, and support of Services.
- Forecast financial requirements; comply with regulatory/legislative requirements.
- If necessary, develop cost recovery procedures that are fair and equitable.

Process (...)	Input from FM to ...	Output from ... to FM
Service Strategy		
Strategy Management for IT Services	• Financial information to influence prioritization of actions/plans • Service investment analysis • Service valuation • ROI/VOI calculations • Cost of StM activities • Budget for strategic plans • Track/report on achievement of strategic objectives (financial view)	• Mission/vision statements • Defines ROI necessary from Service delivery • Defines investment parameters • Resources used in managing the StM process • Proposed process budget
Service Portfolio Management	• Cost of SPM activities • Budget approval • Tools/information to perform ROI calculations • Financial reports • Business case evaluation for new/changed Service (accept/reject decision)	• Service structure which defines cost model, accounting and budgeting system, basis for charging • Service Portfolio • Customer Portfolio • Customer Agreement Portfolio • Project Portfolio • Application Portfolio • Resources used in managing the SPM process • Service packages • Market spaces • Service models

Process (...)	Input from FM to ...	Output from ... to FM
Service Portfolio Management cont.		• Services in pipeline (under review/in development) • Services to be/are retired • Proposed process budget
Demand Management	• Cost of DM • Identify methods to regulate demand (differential charging) • Charging models • Forecast provisioning costs • Costs of differentiated offerings	• Resources used in managing the DM process and activities • Details of predicted PBAs/UPs • Techniques/tools used to manage demand • Proposed process budget
Business Relationship Management	• Cost of BRM • Communicate financial policies and pricing • Arbitrate customers and costs • Service costs • Charging policy • Service valuation • Service investment analysis • ROI/VOI calculations • Incentives/penalties	• Customer Portfolio (which customer is tied (or not) to organization) • How the business measures Service value • What the business is prepared to pay for Services • Resources used in managing the BRM process • Proposed process budget • Proposed usage; customer budget • Agreement to fund/pay for Services
Service Design		
Design Coordination	• Cost of DC • Design criteria for Service value • Current/projected financial requirements for ongoing and new/changed Services • Value proposition	• Proposed process budget • Process costs (Service costing) • Resources used in managing the DC process
Service Catalogue Management	• Cost of SCatM • Cost of Services	• Service Catalogue • Resources used in managing the SCatM process • Proposed process budget
Service Level Management	• Cost of SLM • Service cost • Pricing recommendations • Cost of Service Change • ROI/VOI calculations and interpretations • Cost:Benefit analysis • Financial penalties or incentives • Service Design contribution • Service review contributions • How accounting and charging influence Service use • Charging policies • Validate Service costs • Customer invoices • BIA (financial aspects; AM/ITSCM)	• Service outputs to be costed • Agreed pricing • Resources used in managing the SLM process • Which customers are tied and which untied • Proposed process budget • Service reports

Process (...)	Input from FM to ...	Output from ... to FM
Availability Management	• Cost of AM • Cost of Service unavailability to justify improvements in Availability Plan (e.g. lost user/IT productivity, lost revenue, overtime, wasted goods and materials, fines/penalties, etc.) • Actuarial costs (e.g. loss of customer goodwill/confidence, damage to reputation, loss of business opportunities) • Cost of providing a required level of availability • Budgeted funds for AM purposes (Service Design) • BIA • Cost of Service provision • Cost of Service components • SFA information	• AMIS • Details of any unavailability event • Expenditure justification (design-related, resilience, contract improvements, etc.) • Technical options to meet Service performance • Resources used in managing the AM process • Proposed process budget • Availability Plan • BIA
Capacity Management	• Cost of CapM • Process budget • Assistance in costing Capacity options • Budgeted funds for CapM purposes – Capacity Plan • Financial plans/budgets within BCM and CapM as a unit must coincide with FM practices • Current budget/cost effectiveness • Costs (Service provision, CIs, etc.)	• CMIS (e.g. usage and performance data, etc.) • Resource details to support accounting or charging • Technical options to meet Service performance • Cost allocation methods based on resource usage • Details of predicted PBAs/UPs • Upgrade predictions to support budgeting • Use Moore's Law and Parkinson's Law of Data to support resource procurement • Proposed process budget • Capacity Plan • Predictive/forecast reports • Details to support charging of a new requirement • Cost allocation mechanics based upon resource usage
IT Service Continuity Management	• Cost of ITSCM • Budgeted funds for ITSCM purposes • Evaluation of recovery and Continuity options (costs) • Ensures third party suppliers are paid • Current and future financial plans and strategies • Budgets (ensuring funds for Continuity activities)	• ITSCM Plans (for costing and billing apportionment) • Resources used in managing the ITSCM process • Proposed process budget

Process (...)	Input from FM to ...	Output from ... to FM
IT Service Continuity Management cont.	• Service costs • Apportionment/charging of Services to include Continuity costs	
Information Security Management	• Cost of ISM • Input to business case for new/changed security measures • Financial options on security options	• Security Management Information System (SMIS) • Resources used in managing the ISM process • Proposed process budget • Process activities • Security controls protecting financial data/information
Supplier Management	• Cost of SuppM • Underpinning Contract (UC) cost • Financial penalties or incentives • Policies for contract management • Legislative, regulatory, organizational constraints for contract negotiations and actions • Reports on payments to suppliers • Current IT budgets (overall, by process, by department, by service, etc.) • Standard terms and conditions for payments, etc. • Guidance on purchase and procurement matters	• SCMIS • Resources used in managing the SuppM process • Proposed process budget • Supplier contract performance data
Service Transition		
Transition Planning and Support	• Cost of TPS	• Proposed process budget • Budget/resources for Transition activities • Activity details for Service cost calculations
Change Management	• Cost of ChM • Inputs on financial impact of a RFC • RFC for process improvement • RFC to improve cost effectiveness • Analysis of change costs (proposed vs actual) • CAB member, if needed • Process budget	• Financial assessment of RFCs • CAB minutes • Resources used in managing the ChM process • Proposed process budget • Approved FM process changes
Service Asset and Configuration Management	• CI purchase price, current value, depreciation to date, replacement price, etc.	• CMS/CMDB • Details for cost model development

Process (...)	Input from FM to ...	Output from ... to FM
Service Asset and Configuration Management cont.	• Cost model details • Storing of budgeting and IT accounting information • Charging algorithms • Service Catalogue prices • CI owners • Purchase and upgrade replacement date • Purchase Orders • Acquisitions • Asset register • SACM process budget/cost • Define financial attribute fields (with corporate finance)	• CI relationships for IT accounting • Charging algorithms • CI details (e.g. purchase price, depreciation, replacement, etc.) • CI lifecycle information for replacement budgeting and future planning • Resources used to manage the SACM process • Proposed process budget • Updated information for the asset register • Provides repository to capture cost, depreciation methods, owners, users, maintenance, repair costs, etc.
Release and Deployment Management	• Cost of RDM • Deployment option costs • Analysis of Service asset costs • Procurement of Service assets as needed	• Release Plans (support accounting for new, changed, or retired Service Deployment) • Resources used in managing the RDM process • Proposed process budget
Service Validation and Testing	• Cost of SVT	• Test activities/resources for invoicing/billing/cost of Service • Proposed process budget
Change Evaluation	• Cost of ChE • Cost:Risk analysis	• Resources used in managing the ChE process • Proposed process budget
Knowledge Management	• Cost of KM • Appropriate financial data, information, knowledge • Accurate capture, store, use, and manage process information and data	• Resources used in managing the KM process • Proposed process budget • Relevant, timely, required, and accurate knowledge, information, and data (SKMS)
Service Operation		
Event Management	• Cost of EM • Provide insight into cost for addressing an issue and not addressing an issue	• Resources used to manage the EM process • Proposed process budget
Incident Management	• Cost of IM	• Incident details to assist Service unavailability calculations • Incident details for any FM-related incident (i.e. invoicing, accounting, etc.) • Resources used to manage the IM process • Proposed process budget

Process (...)	Input from FM to ...	Output from ... to FM
Request Fulfillment	• Cost of RF	• Resources used to manage the RF process • Proposed process budget • List of standard Services to be costed
Problem Management	• Cost of PM • Submit possible FM problem for investigation • Resource for PM team • Costing options to remove known problem prior to raising RFC	• Problem details for any FM-related problem (i.e. invoicing, accounting, etc.) • Problem resolution options and benefits for comparative costing • Resources used to manage the PM process • Proposed process budget
Access Management	• Cost of AcM • Cost of access controls	• Resources used to manage the AcM process • Proposed process budget
Continual Service Improvement		
7-step Improvement Process	• Cost of 7S • Identify improvement opportunities • Specific Service improvements based on FM events • Financial analysis of possible improvement options • Budget cycle • Budget/accounting requirements • Flexible commercial models • Data collection on expenditures vs budget • Cost models (service, location, customer, etc.) • Provide financial tracking templates for budgeting and expenditure reports	• Resources used to manage 7S • Approved improvements • CSI Register • Proposed process budget • Improvement possibilities for financial assessment (e.g. ROI/VOI, etc.) • Recommendations for improvement implantation plans

Function (...)	Input from FM to ...	Output from ... to FM
Service Desk	• Approved budget • Function cost	• Call metrics for invoicing/Service cost • Proposed budget
Technical Management	• Approved budget • Function cost/spend	• Information for CAPEX/OPEX planning and spend • Support of underlying technology performing process activities • Participate in regular financial reviews (spend vs budget) • Proposed budgets

Function (...)	Input from FM to ...	Output from ... to FM
Application Management	• Approved budget • Function cost/spend	• Information for CAPEX/OPEX planning and spend • Support of underlying technology performing process activities • Participate in regular financial reviews (spend vs budget) • Proposed budget
IT Operations Management	• Approved budget • Function cost/spend • Financial limitations/constraints for operational Service delivery	• Backup/restore of financial/support data • Printing/document services • Monitoring; data capture • Details of operation services (invoice/billing purposes) • Proposed budget

Demand Management (DM)

Purpose

Identify, predict, and control demand for services; work with CapM to meet demand.

Objectives

- Identify/analyze PBAs to understand service demand.
- Define UPs to understand demand for Service by various user types.
- Ensure Service Designs meet the PBAs and business outcomes.
- Cooperatively work with CapM to ensure adequate resources are available for the Service demand based on PBAs/UPs and there is a balance between cost and Service value.
- Proactively prevent/mitigate demand for Services where capacity resources are limited.
- Effectively manage capacity across all Services to manage and meet changing demand requirements.

Process (...)	Input from DM to ...	Output from ... to DM
Service Strategy		
Strategy Management for IT Services	• PBAs/UPs • Confirmation that current mitigation techniques are in line with Strategy	• Mission/vision statement • Service Strategies • Key business outcomes and business activities (for PBAs/UPs)
Service Portfolio Management	• PBAs/UPs • Differentiated offerings for Service packages • Create/evaluate Service models • Establish/forecast utilization • Identify different types of users • Service package definition • Projected demand for Services/Service packages	• Return of Services currently delivered (understand criticality and impact of Services to organization to manage demand) • Initiate a new/changed Service • Validation of Service models • Validation of Service packages Customer Portfolio • Service Portfolio • Customer Agreement Portfolio
Financial Management	• Resources used in managing the DM process and activities • Details of predicted PBAs/UPs • Techniques/tools used to manage demand • Proposed process budget	• Cost of DM • Identify methods to regulate demand (differential charging) • Charging models • Forecast provisioning costs • Costs of differentiated offerings
Business Relationship Management	• Policies managing demand • Policies to manage under-/over-utilization based on customer estimates • Current mitigation techniques for communication to customers	• Business activities of customer • Validate UPs • Validate differentiated Service offerings • Proposed usage • Service requirements

Process (...)	Input from DM to ...	Output from ... to DM
Business Relationship Management cont.	• PBAs • Differentiated offerings (Service packages)	• Schedules of customer activity • Reports of customer perception
Service Design		
Design Coordination	• Demand mitigation techniques currently used (ensure designs will be able to incorporate if necessary) • PBAs/UPs • Differentiated Service offering options	
Service Catalogue Management	• Mitigation techniques as a possible addition to Service description • Define Service packages (with SPM)	
Service Level Management	• PBAs/UPs • Methods to deal with supply/demand variance • Actual utilization/performance levels	• Formal agreement with customer on utilization levels • Service reports (usage changes, breaches) • Assist in predictive business behavior (develop PBAs, UPs) • Service details to assist DM techniques
Availability Management	• PBAs (understand critical Service availability) • UPs • DM techniques	• Service Outage Analysis (SOA) • Projected Service availability • Availability Plan
Capacity Management	• Policies for management of demand when resources are over-utilized • How to match supply/demand in design and operation of the Service • DM techniques/restrictions • PBAs/UPs (performance, utilization, throughput, etc.)	• How to match supply/demand in design and operation of the Service • Monitor actual utilization • Interpret utilization trends
IT Service Continuity Management	• PBAs/UPs • Sizing recovery options	• BIA
Information Security Management	• Current mitigation techniques to ensure no breach in security protocols • UPs	• Results of security assessment on mitigation techniques • Security Policy
Supplier Management	• PBAs/UPs	• "On demand" contract conditions based on Capacity Plan/DM techniques

Process (...)	Input from DM to ...	Output from ... to DM
Service Transition		
Transition Planning and Support	• Long-term information around resource requirements	
Change Management	• Assess impact of changes on how business uses a Service • RFC for improved process	• Initiate process activities for new/changed Services which required demand techniques
Service Asset and Configuration Management	• PBAs/UPs (document CI)	• Identify relationship between Service demand and demand on systems/devices
Release and Deployment Management	• Impact of Release Plan on current demand constraints	• Release Plans
Service Validation and Testing	• Proposed/known Service resource limits • Techniques used to be included in testing	• Validate PBAs via testing • Validate methods of preventing over-utilization of resources • Request for input to test scenarios for managing future demand
Change Evaluation		• Recommendations on demand based on change trends
Knowledge Management	• Accurate capture, store, use, and manage process information and data	• Relevant, timely, required, and accurate knowledge, information, and data
Service Operation		
Event Management	• Monitoring thresholds to prevent demand-related events	• Provide actual Service utilization via monitoring • Validate PBAs • Event information as it relates to PBAs
Incident Management	• Possible mitigation for demand-related incident	• Demand-related incidents
Request Fulfillment	•	• Usage of RF system (total number of hits and breakdown by request)
Problem Management	• Demand-related data for problem investigation/actions	• Demand-related problems • Workarounds for demand-related issues
Access Management		• Access granted per Service
Continual Service Improvement		
7-step Improvement Process	• Identify improvement opportunities • Specific Service improvements based on demand-related events	• Communication of improvement initiatives • Recommendations for improvement implantation plans

Function (...)	Input from DM to ...	Output from ... to DM
Service Desk	• Information on constraint technology applied (justification)	• Complaints • Information on performance issues/errors from constraints
Technical Management	• DM techniques to apply	• Deploy technical constraints • Reports on affect
Application Management	• DM techniques to apply	• Deploy technical constraints • Reports on affect
IT Operations Management		• Reports on affect

Business Relationship Management (BRM)

Purpose

Create/maintain a business relationship between the Service Provider and customer; strategically and tactically manage customer needs against Service Provider capabilities.

Objectives

- Ensure the customer view of a Service is understood by the Service Provider (e.g. its criticality, value, features/capabilities, etc.).
- Ensure customer satisfaction (Service Provider meets customer needs) and manage the relationship to that end.
- Communicate change (e.g. customer, technology, organizational, etc.) that could impact Service delivery.
- Communicate new requirements for existing or new Services.
- Confirm business needs, as defined by the customer, are met and that Services delivered provide value to the customer.
- Mediate the Service Provider–customer relationship, when necessary.
- Create/maintain a complaints/escalation process for the customer.

Process (…)	Input from BRM to …	Output from … to BRM
Service Strategy		
Strategy Management for IT Services	<ul><li>Information about the customer (e.g. objectives, environment, requirements)</li><li>Defined business outcomes</li><li>Customer Portfolio</li><li>Validates changes of requirement, design, funding, design model, or strategy to the overall Service Strategy</li></ul>	<ul><li>Mission/vision</li><li>Service strategies</li><li>Policies</li><li>Strategic plans, perspectives, policies</li><li>Business outcomes met by various Services</li></ul>
Service Portfolio Management	<ul><li>Initiate Request for new/changed Services</li><li>Provide business information</li><li>Service requirements</li><li>Business requirements (objectives, outcomes, priorities)</li><li>Customer Portfolio</li><li>Customer Agreement Portfolio (SLM)</li><li>Suggestions or complaints</li><li>Business case evaluation for new/changed Service (accept/reject decision)</li><li>Market space suggestions</li><li>Business case for a new/changing Service</li></ul>	<ul><li>Up-to-date Service Portfolio</li><li>Service models</li><li>Market spaces</li><li>Application Portfolio</li><li>Project Portfolio</li><li>Service charters</li><li>Service proposals</li><li>Status reports on new/changed Services</li><li>Business case evaluation for new/changed Service (accept/reject decision)</li></ul>

Process (...)	Input from BRM to ...	Output from ... to BRM
Financial Management	• Customer Portfolio (which customer is tied (or not) to organization) • How the business measures Service value • What the business is prepared to pay for Services • Resources used in managing the BRM process • Proposed process budget • Proposed usage; customer budget • Agreement to fund/pay for Services	• Cost of BRM • Communicate financial policies and pricing • Arbitrate customers and costs • Service costs • Charging policy • Service valuation • Service investment analysis • ROI/VOI calculations • Incentives/penalties
Demand Management	• Business activities of customer • Validate UPs • Validate differentiated Service offerings • Proposed usage • Service requirements • Schedules of customer activity • Reports of customer perception	• Policies managing demand • Policies to manage under-/over-utilization based on customer estimates • Current mitigation techniques for communication to customers • PBAs • Differentiated offerings (Service packages)
Service Design		
Design Coordination	• Customer desires in terms of utility/warranty • Change in business requirements • Customer needs and priorities • Business outcomes • Customer activity schedule (assist in planning the designs – when can a customer participate, etc.) • Training and awareness scheduling	• Comprehensive/consistent Service Design meeting requirements (SDP)
Service Catalogue Management	• Service stakeholders • Agreed business requirements • Agreed Service levels (warranty) • Information for Service description	• Service description (ensure accuracy)
Service Level Management	• Customer Portfolio • Customer needs (utility/warranty) • High-level customer/Service requirements • Service improvement opportunities • Stakeholders	• Tactical and operational relationship with the customer • Customer Agreement Portfolio • SQP • Service reports • SLRs, SLAs, OLAs • Service Improvement Plans (SIPs)

Process (...)	Input from BRM to ...	Output from ... to BRM
Service Level Management cont.	• Expectation management • Strategic and tactical relationship with the customer • Customer business calendar • Business information (strategic, tactical, operational, financial, etc.) • Customer (dis-)satisfaction • Service review meetings • Manage complaints/compliments • Customer engagement, when necessary	• Service reports (performance vs targets) • PSO • Confirmation of Service availability requirements for a new/changed Service • Manage complaints/compliments
Availability Management	• Usage (Availability Plan) • Potential Service targets • Schedules of customer activity (for testing, maintenance, etc.) • Projected Service Outage (PSO) agreement • Service Acceptance Criteria (SAC) • Customer requirements • Change requirements • Service review • Forecasts of usage	• Agreed requirements/designs • Agreed Service targets • Reports on availability • Prevented incidents (proactive, mitigation on account of design, etc.) • SFA report/outcome • Availability accomplishments
Capacity Management	• Projected Service usage/consumption (Capacity Plan)	• Reports on capacity (workload, usage, forecasts, etc.)
IT Service Continuity Management	• Business Continuity Plan (BCP) requirements • Provides definition of "disaster" (customer view) • Service priorities/criticality • Assurance of business awareness of ITSCM Plans/measures • Discussion of Continuity planning with customers • Validation that Continuity measures are valid for current environment • Recovery criteria	• Communicate change in risk or impact to business processes • ITSCM Plans • ITSCM Testing Schedule (for customer involvement) • BIA outcome • ITSCM test reports
Information Security Management	• Security requirements • Business plans (current/future) • Legislative/regulatory requirements • Business needs	• Change in risk or mitigation methods (communicate to customer) • Reports on security (breaches, controls, etc.)
Supplier Management	• Service requirements • Complaints/compliments • New/changed business needs • Satisfaction survey results	• UCs

Process (...)	Input from BRM to ...	Output from ... to BRM
Service Transition		
Transition Planning and Support	• Customer response from Communication Plan • Service requirements	• Transition Plans • Communication Plan • Requests for customer resources for Transition activities (e.g. testing, evaluation, pilot, etc.)
Change Management	• Change proposal • Service charter • Service requirements • Participation in CAB/PIR • Potential risk to customer business from a proposed change • Business impact/urgency information • Schedules of customer activity • Schedules of training and awareness events • RFC for process improvements	• Approved changes, charters, proposals • Status of changes • Change Schedule • PSO • Ensured testing • Ensured remediation planning
Service Asset and Configuration Management	• Stakeholders • Service customers	• Critical documents (e.g. history, data, etc.) held within the CMDB
Release and Deployment Management	• Defined business outcomes • Service requirements • Schedule of customer activity • Schedule of training and awareness events • Input when establishing Release policies to ensure policies reflect business need • Input during planning to ensure business operations are not negatively impacted during a release	• New/changed Service Deployment • Service notification • Release Policy • Release Plan
Service Validation and Testing	• SAC • Customer requirements • Confirmation of test requirements	• Results of user acceptance testing (UAT)
Change Evaluation	• Customer risk information • Customer requirements • Request by stakeholder for Evaluation • Impact assessment of issues identified from Evaluation • Customers/users to participate in Evaluation activities, if needed	• Resource for answers to customer/user questions around Evaluation activities of new/changed Service • Interim/final Evaluation reports (to report to customer)
Knowledge Management	• Knowledge capture around customer/business requirements	• Relevant, timely, required, and accurate knowledge, information, and data (SKMS)

Process (...)	Input from BRM to ...	Output from ... to BRM
Knowledge Management cont.	• Accurate capture, store, use, and manage process information and data • Store minutes of customer meeting	
Service Operation		
Event Management		
Incident Management	• Customer satisfaction requirements • Customer perception • Complaints/compliments	• Satisfaction survey results • Prevented incidents (proactive work)
Request Fulfillment	• Customer satisfaction requirements • Customer perception	• Satisfaction survey results • Use of the RF system
Problem Management	• Customer satisfaction requirements • Customer perception	• Prevented outages (proactive work)
Access Management	• Projected user community	• Reports on rights granted or rejected • Reports on unauthorized Service access attempts • Reports on Service access breaches
Continual Service Improvement		
7-step Improvement Process	• Confirmation of improvements (business benefit) • Specific Service improvements based on BRM events • Business plans and strategy • Service review meetings • Customer satisfaction surveys • New business requirements • Report format • Customer Portfolio • Customer Agreement Portfolio (SLM) • Complaints/compliments • Identify improvement opportunities	• Data analysis • Reports based on requests • Monitoring/measuring capability • Service improvement opportunities • Agreed improvements (pending ChM) • Recommendations for improvement implantation plans

Function (...)	Input from BRM to ...	Output from ... to BRM
Service Desk	• Customer satisfaction information • Complaints/compliments	• Performance metrics for review meetings (indicating Service achievements)
Technical Management		• Support of underlying technology for process activities • Capabilities/resources
Application Management		• Support of underlying technology for process activities • Capabilities/resources
IT Operations Management	• Complaints/compliments on standard operational Services	• Support of underlying technology for process activities • Capabilities/resources

Service Design (SD)

Purpose

Take a holistic view of Service Design (e.g. Service solution, architecture, processes, policies, metrics, etc.) in order to achieve the defined Strategy, value requirements, and business outcomes.

Objectives

- "Get the design correct the first time," meaning minimal retroactive improvements (i.e. poor requirements gathering) over the lifecycle of the Service.
- Design to aid continual improvement caused by changing technologies, business direction, etc.

Lifecycle stage (...)	Input from SD to ...	Output from ... to SD
Service Strategy	<ul><li>Input to business cases and the Service Portfolio</li><li>SDPs</li><li>Updated Service models</li><li>Service Portfolio updates including the Service Catalogue</li><li>Financial estimates and reports</li><li>Design-related knowledge and information in the SKMS</li><li>Designs for SS processes and procedures</li></ul>	<ul><li>Vision and mission</li><li>Service Portfolio</li><li>Policies</li><li>Strategies and strategic plans</li><li>Priorities</li><li>Service charters including Service packages and details of utility and warranty</li><li>Financial information and budgets</li><li>Documented PBAs and UPs</li><li>Service models</li></ul>
Service Transition	<ul><li>Service Catalogue</li><li>SDPs, including:<ul><li>Details of utility and warranty</li><li>Acceptance criteria</li><li>Service models</li><li>Designs and interface specifications</li><li>Transition plans</li><li>Operation plans and procedures</li></ul></li><li>RFCs to transition or deploy new or changed Services</li><li>Input to Change evaluation and CAB meetings</li><li>Designs for ST processes and procedures</li><li>SLAs, OLAs, and UCs</li></ul>	<ul><li>Service Catalogue updates</li><li>Feedback on all aspects of Service Design and SDPs</li><li>Input and feedback to Transition plans</li><li>Response to RFCs</li><li>Knowledge and information in the SKMS (including the CMS)</li><li>Design errors identified in Transition for re-design</li><li>Evaluation reports</li></ul>

Lifecycle stage (...)	Input from SD to ...	Output from ... to SD

Service Operation	• Service Catalogue
	• SDP, including:
	  ○ Details of utility and warranty
	  ○ Operations plans and procedures
	  ○ Recovery procedures
	• Knowledge and information in the SKMS
	• Vital business functions
	• HW/SW maintenance requirements
	• Designs for Service operation processes and procedures
	• SLAs, OLAs, UCs
	• Security policies
		• Operational requirements
		• Actual performance information
		• RFCs to resolve operational issues
		• Historical incident and problem records

Continual Service Improvement	• Service Catalogue • SDPs including details of utility and warranty • Knowledge and information in the SKMS • Achievements against metrics, KPIs and CSFs • Design of Services; measurements; processes; infrastructure; systems • Design for the 7S improvement process and procedures • Improvement opportunities logged in the CSI register	• Results of customer and user satisfaction surveys • Input to design requirements • Data required for metrics, KPIs and CSFs • Service reports • Feedback on SDPs • RFCs for implementing improvements

From: *ITIL® Service Design*, Table 3.7. ©Crown copyright 2011. Reproduced under license from the Cabinet Office.

Design Coordination (DC)

Purpose

Ensure Service Design phase goals and objectives are met by acting as a single point of contact for all activities and processes within Service Design.

Objectives

- Ensure a consistent, repeatable design process that incorporates services, management system, architecture, technology, processes, measures, and information that meets current and future business objectives.
- Activity coordination across all aspects of the design phase, including resource conflict resolution.
- Resource and capability planning and coordination.
- SDP production.
- Hand-off of SDPs/designs to ST, as agreed.
- Management of hand-offs between SS and ST ensuring quality criteria and maintaining requirement integrity.
- Ensure SDPs/designs meet strategic, architectural, governance, and organizational requirements and standards.
- Improve effectiveness and efficiency of the phase activities/processes.

Process (...)	Input from DC to ...	Output from ... to DC
Service Strategy		
Strategy Management for IT Services	• Plans/designs that address (meet) the strategic objectives (SDP)	• Mission/vision • Service Strategy • Defines policies that must be met when designing Services • Definition of what design efforts require DC efforts • Defines constraints that must be addressed by designs • Defines specific outcomes Services need to achieve • Service charter • Service models • Governance policies • Legal, regulatory, statutory requirements
Service Portfolio Management	• SDP • Service Portfolio updates • Updated Service models • Project updates	• Service Portfolio • Service charter • Change proposal • Business case • Business requirements • Design work prioritized to business need • How the Service will be measured by the business

Process (...)	Input from DC to ...	Output from ... to DC
Service Portfolio Management cont.		• Linkage between Service component/asset and business outcome • Market space information • Utility/warranty requirements • Service options • Risks • Priorities • Project Portfolio (PMO)
Financial Management	• Proposed process budget • Process costs (Service costing) • Resources used in managing the DC process	• Cost of DC • Design criteria for Service value • Current/projected financial requirements for ongoing and new/changed Services • Value proposition
Demand Management		• Demand mitigation techniques currently used (ensure designs will be able to incorporate if necessary) • PBAs/UPs • Differentiated Service offering options
Business Relationship Management	• Comprehensive/consistent Service Design meeting requirements (SDP)	• Change in business requirements • Customer needs and priorities • Business outcomes • Customer activity schedule (assist in planning the designs – when can a customer participate, etc.) • Training and awareness scheduling
Service Design		
Service Catalogue Management	• New/changed Service information	• Service Catalogue
Service Level Management	• Templates and standards to assist in consistent and accurate data capture • Status reports	• SQP • Define/agree SLRs • Service targets • Change in business requirements
Availability Management	• Policies, guidelines, standards, budgets, models, resources, and capabilities • Document templates • Documentation plans • Training plans • Communication/marketing plans	• Risk assessment • Availability requirements/designs to be included in the SDP • Availability Plan

Process (...)	Input from DC to ...	Output from ... to DC
Availability Management cont.	• Measurement/metrics plans • Testing plans • Deployment plans • Scheduling • Conflict resolution (resources) • Review, measurement, improvement suggestions • Review of designs ensuring requirements are addressed (utility and warranty) • Requirements	
Capacity Management	• Policies, guidelines, standards, budgets, models, resources, and capabilities • Document templates • Documentation plans • Training plans • Communication/marketing plans • Measurement/metrics plans • Testing plans • Deployment plans • Scheduling • Conflict resolution (resources) • Review, measurement, improvement suggestions • Review of designs ensuring requirements are addressed (utility and warranty)	• Capacity requirements/designs to be included in the SDP
IT Service Continuity Management	• Policies, guidelines, standards, budgets, models, resources, and capabilities • Document templates • Documentation plans • Training plans • Communication/marketing plans • Measurement/metrics plans • Testing plans • Deployment plans • Scheduling • Conflict resolution (resources) • Review, measurement, improvement suggestions • Review of designs ensuring requirements are addressed (utility and warranty) • Designs/plans for new/changed Services for review/agreement	• Continuity requirements/designs to be included in the SDP
Information Security Management	• Policies, guidelines, standards, budgets, models, resources, and capabilities	• Information security requirements/designs to be included in the SDP

Process (...)	Input from DC to ...	Output from ... to DC
Information Security Management cont.	• Document templates • Documentation plans • Training plans • Communication/marketing plans • Measurement/metrics plans • Testing plans • Deployment plans • Scheduling • Conflict resolution (resources) • Review, measurement, improvement suggestions • Review of designs ensuring requirements are addressed (utility and warranty)	• Security Policy (ensure all designs conform to its requirements)
Supplier Management	• Shared and agreed practices to support process activities and the overall Service Design • Information pertinent to contract review to support design activities • New/changed designs	• Supplier risk management • Shared and agreed practices to support process activities and the overall Service Design • Supplier and/or contract information pertinent to Service Design activities
Service Transition		
Transition Planning and Support	• Complete SDP (Service charter, Service specifications, Service models, architectural design, definition/design of each associated release with associated entry/exit criteria, assembly Service components for the release package, RDM plans, SAC, etc.) • Shared and agreed practices to ensure a smooth transfer between design and Transition activities	• Shared and agreed practices to ensure a smooth transfer between design and Transition activities
Change Management	• Updated change records • Status information on design activities • RFC for process improvements	• Definition of which design efforts require DC efforts • Change in business requirements • RFCs • Change records • Authorized changes • Change Schedule • Change records • PIR minutes (improvements to DC activities)
Service Asset and Configuration Management	• SDPs	• CMS, CMDB

Process (...)	Input from DC to ...	Output from ... to DC
Release and Deployment Management	• Ensure planning and design of Release units and Deployment actions are integrated into overall design (SDP)	• Plan/design of Release and Deployment of new/changed Service for inclusion to the SDP
Service Validation and Testing	• Ensure planning and design of tests are integrated into overall design (SDP) • SDP (Service charter, Service provide interface definitions, operation models, capacity/resource model/plans, financial models (TCO, TCU, etc.), SM model, test conditions (expected results), design/interface specifications, Release/Deployment plans, acceptance criteria)	• Plan/design of Service test requirements for inclusion to the SDP • Test capabilities/resources
Change Evaluation	• SDP (Service charter, SAC, etc.) • Ensure SDP contains accurate and up-to-date information to assist ChE activities	• Evaluation of SD activities (how well it meets stated requirements)
Knowledge Management	• Accurate capture, store, use and manage process information and data • Update of SDP • Knowledge, information, and data around the new/changed Service to be included and managed within the SKMS	• Relevant, timely, required, and accurate knowledge, information, and data
Service Operation		
Event Management		
Incident Management		• Incidents that relate to the design of a Service
Request Fulfillment		
Problem Management		• Problems that relate to the design of a Service
Access Management	• Requests for access to design data, tools, etc. for staff (new and outgoing, etc.)	

Process (...)	Input from DC to ...	Output from ... to DC
Continual Service Improvement		
7-step Improvement Process	• Proposed improvements to process and design activities • Specific Service improvements based on DC event(s) • SDP • Ensure monitoring/measuring criteria are included in designs • Ensure CSFs/KPIs are measurable and effective	• Assessed improvements (accepted or rejected) • Service improvement opportunities • Business case

Function (...)	Input from DC to ...	Output from ... to DC
Service Desk		
Technical Management		• Define standards for designing new architecture • Participate in plan/design activities for new/changed Services
Application Management		• Participate in plan/design activities for new/changed Services • Information from related applications that may impact new/changed Services
IT Operations Management		

Service Catalogue Management (SCatM)

Purpose

Provide a single source of consistent information available to all who are authorized to access it on all operational Services or those ready to be deployed.

Objectives

- Manage the information within the Service Catalogue ensuring accuracy (e.g. details, status, interfaces, dependencies, etc.) and relevancy.
- Ensure the Service Catalogue is available in a format that is appropriate to those authorized to access it.

Process (...)	Input from SCatM to ...	Output from ... to SCatM
Service Strategy		
Strategy Management for IT Services	• Up-to-date Service Catalogue	• Mission/vision • Service Strategy • Policies
Service Portfolio Management	• Service definition • Service Portfolio updates (ensures Service Catalogue and Portfolio "agree") • Builds and maintains the Service Catalogue	• Service charter • Change proposals • Determines which Services and Service packages to include in the Service Catalogue • Information to include in Service descriptions/Service Catalogue • Service packages
Financial Management	• Service Catalogue • Resources used in managing process activities • Proposed process budget	• Cost of SCatM • Cost of Services
Demand Management		• Mitigation techniques as a possible addition to Service description • Defines Service packages (with SPM)
Business Relationship Management	• Service description (ensure accuracy)	• Service stakeholders • Agreed business requirements • Agreed Service levels (warranty) • Information for Service description

Process (...)	Input from SCatM to ...	Output from ... to SCatM
Service Design		
Design Coordination	• Service Catalogue	• New/changed Service information
Service Level Management	• Service Catalogue • Service definition • Service users	• Agreed business requirements • Agreed Service levels (warranty) • Service information for Service Catalogue entry
Availability Management	• Service information	
Capacity Management		
IT Service Continuity Management	• Service Catalogue	• Continuity information to be included in the Service description
Information Security Management	• Service Catalogue	• Security information for Service description
Supplier Management	• Service Catalogue	
Service Transition		
Transition Planning and Support		• Communication Plan (adding new/changed Service to Service Catalogue)
Change Management	• RFC updates (impact to Service description/information) • RFC for process improvements	• Approved Service Catalogue changes
Service Asset and Configuration Management	• Service Catalogue for Service CI definition (include in CMS; link CIs)	• CMDB identifies all items within a Service, which might be helpful in developing a Service Catalogue
Release and Deployment Management	• Service Catalogue (to understand the overall nature of all Services)	• Information on deployed changes to a Service in the Service Catalogue (update information for the Service)
Service Validation and Testing		
Change Evaluation	• Services in the Service Catalogue and impact criteria for the Services	
Knowledge Management	• Accurate capture, store, use, and manage process information and data • Updated Service Catalogue	• Relevant, timely, required, and accurate knowledge, information, and data • Standards for managing the information regarding the Services in the Service Catalogue

Process (…)	Input from SCatM to …	Output from … to SCatM
Service Operation		
Event Management		
Incident Management	• Services available to which customers and/or profiles	• Incidents related to the use of the Service Catalogue • Incidents related to the information in the Service Catalogue
Request Fulfillment	• Published Service Requests	• Information regarding Service Requests to be published by SCatM
Problem Management	• Problems regarding the Service	• Workarounds for known errors in the Service Catalogue
Access Management		• Information (requirements) for getting access to Services
Continual Service Improvement		
7-step Improvement Process	• Service Catalogue • Identify improvement opportunities • Specific Service improvements based on Service Catalogue events	• Communication of improvement initiatives • Update to Service description • Recommendations for improvement implantation plans

Function (…)	Input from SCatM to …	Output from … to SCatM
Service Desk	• Service Catalogue	
Technical Management		
Application Management		
IT Operations Management		

Service Level Management (SLM)

Purpose

All current and agreed Services are delivered to the agreed achievable targets.

Objectives

- Define, negotiate, document, agree, monitor, measure, review, report, and improve Services.
- Manage and improve the customer relationship/communication at an operational/tactical level (BRM).
- Ensure Service targets are measurable.
- Manage customer satisfaction (BRM) via delivered Service quality (as defined by the customer).
- Manage customer expectation via clear and unambiguous Service description and Service performance targets.
- Proactively and cost-effectively improve Services.

Process (...)	Input from SLM to ...	Output from ... to SLM
Service Strategy		
Strategy Management for IT Services	<ul><li>Customer Agreement Portfolio</li><li>Service reports (achievement of strategic objectives)</li><li>SQP</li><li>Results of Service reviews/improvements</li></ul>	<ul><li>Mission/vision</li><li>Service Strategy</li><li>Policies</li><li>Strategy requirements for new/changed Services</li><li>Project Portfolio (owned by PMO)</li><li>Constraints</li></ul>
Service Portfolio Management	<ul><li>Manages Services to achieve agreed Service levels</li><li>Reports on achieved Service levels</li><li>Customer Agreement Portfolio</li><li>Service reports (achievement of business outcome)</li></ul>	<ul><li>Portfolio, Pipeline, Retired Services</li><li>Customer Portfolio</li><li>Customer Agreement Portfolio</li><li>Application Portfolio</li><li>Project Portfolio (PMO)</li><li>Service models</li><li>Market spaces</li><li>Strategic risks</li></ul>
Financial Management	<ul><li>Service outputs to be costed</li><li>Agreed pricing</li><li>Resources used in managing the SLM process</li><li>Which customers are tied and which untied</li><li>Proposed process budget</li><li>Service reports</li></ul>	<ul><li>Cost of SLM</li><li>Service cost</li><li>Pricing recommendations</li><li>Cost of Service Change</li><li>ROI/VOI calculations and interpretations</li><li>Cost:Benefit analysis</li><li>Financial penalties or incentives</li><li>Service Design contribution</li><li>Service review contributions</li><li>How accounting and charging influence Service use</li></ul>

Process (...)	Input from SLM to ...	Output from ... to SLM
Financial Management cont.		• Charging policies • Validate Service costs • Customer invoices • BIA (financial aspects; AM/ITSCM)
Demand Management	• Formal agreement with customer on utilization levels • Service reports (usage changes, breaches) • Assist in predictive business behavior (develop PBAs, UPs) • Service details to assist DM techniques	• PBAs/UPs • Methods to deal with supply/demand variance • Actual utilization/performance levels
Business Relationship Management	• Tactical and operational relationship with the customer • Customer Agreement Portfolio • SQP • Service reports • SLRs, SLAs, OLAs • SIPs • Service reports (performance vs targets) • PSO • Confirmation of Service availability requirements for a new/changed Service • Manage complaints/compliments	• Customer Portfolio • Customer needs (utility/warranty) • High-level customer/Service requirements • Service improvement opportunities • Stakeholders • Expectation management • Strategic and tactical relationship with the customer • Customer business calendar • Business information (strategic, tactical, operational, financial, etc.) • Customer (dis-)satisfaction • Service review meetings • Manage complaints/compliments • Customer engagement, when necessary
Service Design		
Design Coordination	• SQP • Define/agree SLRs • Service targets • Change in business requirements	• Templates and standards to assist in consistent and accurate data capture • Status reports
Service Catalogue Management	• Agreed business requirements • Agreed Service levels (warranty) • Service information for Service Catalogue entry	• Service Catalogue • Service definition • Service users
Availability Management	• Confirmation of Service availability requirements for a new/changed Service • SIPs	• BIA • Define/agree realistic Service targets

Process (...)	Input from SLM to ...	Output from ... to SLM
Availability Management cont.	<ul><li>Ensures participation of availability in SLR > SLA negotiations</li><li>Service Information (monitoring)</li><li>Service requirements and targets</li><li>Service reviews</li><li>Usage forecasts</li><li>Determine/validate Service targets</li><li>SFA information</li></ul>	<ul><li>Availability reports (trend/future requirements; performance) for Service review meetings</li><li>Availability Plan</li><li>Improvement actions for SIP</li><li>Input to Cost:Value ratio</li><li>Risk assessment</li><li>Service Designs to meet recoverability requirements</li><li>Service monitoring</li></ul>
Capacity Management	<ul><li>SIPs</li><li>BCM information</li><li>SCM information</li><li>Assists in identifying and predicting the behavior of the business drivers of capacity</li><li>Details of Services to be considered if DM invoked</li><li>Capacity target validation</li><li>Capacity-related Service breach data</li></ul>	<ul><li>Capacity Plan</li><li>Define/agree realistic Service targets</li><li>Identification of throughput and peaks and troughs for SLAs Reports for Service review meetings</li><ul><li>Trend/usage</li><li>Resource (technology, human, etc.) limitations</li><li>Identify data for SLA reviews (batch jobs, response times, etc.)</li><li>Service-based reports</li><li>Exception reports</li></ul></ul>
IT Service Continuity Management	<ul><li>SLRs and SLAs in DR situations</li><li>Details of all "standard" SLA requirements</li><li>Service priorities to check against customer view</li><li>Agreed levels of Service to be provided in a disaster</li><li>Review of tests</li><li>Assurance of business awareness</li><li>Assurance that OLAs/UCs include support required for ITSCM</li><li>New/changed Service targets</li><li>SLAs (Continuity targets and standard details)</li><li>Service priorities/criticality</li><li>Test result review (meets agreed parameters)</li><li>Assurance of customer awareness of responsibilities and IT measures/activities</li><li>Agreed Continuity testing timetables (SLAs)</li><li>Monitor/review/report on Service targets after invocation of the ITSCM Plan</li></ul>	<ul><li>BIA</li><li>Define/agree realistic Service targets/levels during Continuity event</li><li>Capabilities for Continuity actions</li><li>Risk assessment</li><li>ITSCM Plan (for reference within SLAs) with confirmed actions</li></ul>

Process (...)	Input from SLM to ...	Output from ... to SLM
Information Security Management	<ul><li>Security requirements</li><li>Service information</li><li>Service monitoring information</li><li>Service breaches</li><li>Investigation/reporting on security events</li></ul>	<ul><li>Assist in security requirement negotiations</li><li>Define/agree realistic Service targets</li></ul>
Supplier Management	<ul><li>SLR for contract negotiations</li><li>Policy for shared activities</li><li>Manage complaints/compliments</li><li>New/changed Service requirements</li><li>Negotiation assistance</li><li>Definition of Service targets</li><li>Investigation of SLA/SLR breaches due to poor supplier performance</li><li>Information for SuppM review process</li><li>Assistance in contract management, if necessary</li></ul>	<ul><li>UCs</li><li>Policy for shared activities</li><li>Contract performance</li><li>Contract changes</li><li>Manage complaints/compliments</li><li>Supplier Policy</li><li>Supplier performance information (potentially)</li></ul>
Service Transition		
Transition Planning and Support	<ul><li>SLRs/SLAs</li><li>Transition-related process activity results included in updated SDP</li></ul>	<ul><li>Communication Plan</li></ul>
Change Management	<ul><li>PSO negotiation and agreement</li><li>RFCs for new/changed Services</li><li>Service levels to assist in classifying changes</li><li>CAB/ECAB attendance, as appropriate</li><li>RFCs for process improvement</li><li>Passes user generated RFCs for analysis</li><li>Attend CAB</li><li>Assesses potential impact of changes on Service quality (disruption of agreed availability/performance, etc.)</li><li>Prioritization based on OLAs (IT capabilities) and Service criticality (customer and BRM input)</li><li>Impact of RFC on current customers/services (e.g. quality, agreed Service delivery, etc.)</li><li>SIPs</li><li>RFC for process improvements</li></ul>	<ul><li>CAB agenda/minutes</li><li>PSO agreement</li><li>RFCs</li><li>Change Schedule</li><li>Information concerning performance of change both when implemented and subsequently</li><li>Receives regular change performance reports</li><li>Remediation reports</li></ul>

Process (...)	Input from SLM to ...	Output from ... to SLM
Service Asset and Configuration Management	• Service information • SLRs, SLAs, OLAs, SIPs. SLAM documents to be included as CIs • Relationships between SLAs/OLAs/UCs, etc... • Information on access to CI records	• Relationships between Services, Service assets, CIs and customers • Holds SLM documents as CIs • CMDB useful when developing improvement plans • Shows components within a Service which may help justify Service costs • CMDB useful in developing SIP
Release and Deployment Management	• SLRs (input when establishing Release policies) • Confirmation that defined users are available for implementation and/or distribution of a release, as planned and agreed	• Release policies • Release Plans • Information to update SLAs/OLAs • Information to update Service reports • Request for users in UAT testing
Service Validation and Testing	• Service targets (as test targets)	
Change Evaluation	• Impact assessment of issues identified from Evaluation • Customers/users to participate in Evaluation activities, if needed	• Resource for answer customer/user questions around Evaluation activities of new/changed Service
Knowledge Management	• Accurate capture, store, use and manage process information and data • Store minutes of customer meeting • Service review meeting minutes • Customer report	• Relevant, timely, required and accurate knowledge, information and data • Expectations of maintaining any Service-related knowledge
Service Operation		
Event Management	• Priority and impact of an event based on SLA targets • SLRs	• Monitoring activities (Service achievements, proactive prevention of failure, etc.) • Service failure • Service threshold alerts indicating a potential breach of SLA/OLA requirement (proactive expectation management)
Incident Management	• SQP • Agreed Service levels/targets • Thresholds for addressing incidents • Prioritization based on OLAs (IT capabilities) and Service criticality (customer and BRM input)	• Recommendations for updates to incident thresholds • Service outages/incidents • IM capabilities as input to OLAs/Service expectations • Potential Service failure information

Process (...)	Input from SLM to ...	Output from ... to SLM
Incident Management cont.	• Service level to assist in classifying incidents	• Escalation information • Restoration information • Survey results (by Service Desk staff) • Complaints/compliments • Service terms (conditions that can be met by IM staff) • Measures of Service achievements (agreed metrics/measures)
Request Fulfillment	• Service targets for fulfillment activities	• Performance reports
Problem Management	• SIPs • Service levels to assist in classifying problems • Prioritization based on OLAs (IT capabilities) and Service criticality (customer and BRM input) • Highlights potential problems • Resource into problem resolution teams	• Reports on problem activities • Potential threats to Service levels • Proactive prevention for achievement of Service targets
Access Management	• SLRs/SLAs containing requirements for managing access to the Service	• Reports on unauthorized Service access attempts • Reports on Service access breaches
Continual Service Improvement		
7-step Improvement Process	• SIP • SQP • Specific Service improvements based on SLM events • Service review meetings • Updates SLAM chart, scorecards, etc. • Service level targets • Service level analysis • SLAs, OLAs to meet needs and capabilities • Defines what is measured and reported via negotiations with the business • Ensures all agreed measures (SLAs) are actually measurable • Complaints/compliments • Identify improvement opportunities	• CSI Register • Process improvement opportunities • Agreed Service improvements • Updated/addressed SIP(s) • Recommendations for improvement implantation plans

Function (...)	Input from SLM to ...	Output from ... to SLM
Service Desk	• SLAs • Request for customer satisfaction survey	• Complaints/compliments • Service performance information • Improvement opportunities
Technical Management	• OLAs	• Resources/capabilities for OLAs
Application Management	• OLAs	• Resources/capabilities for OLAs
IT Operations Management	• OLAs	• Monitoring activities • Resources/capabilities for OLAs

Availability Management (AM)

Purpose

Ensures the agreed level of Service availability is met cost-effectively, both now and in the future.

Objectives

- Produce and maintain an Availability Plan.
- Provide guidance and support on all availability-related matters (e.g. incidents, problems, etc.).
- Manage Service and component availability to ensure agreed Service targets are met.
- Assess RFCs for availability impact to the Availability Plan and current Service delivery.
- Proactive cost-justified availability improvements.

Process (...)	Input from AM to ...	Output from ... to AM
Service Strategy		
Strategy Management for IT Services	• Availability Plan • Designs meeting strategic requirements • Links Service Designs to business outcomes • Proactive AM measures • Risk assessment and countermeasures	• Mission/vision • Service Strategy • Policies • Strategy requirements for new/changed Services • Project Portfolio (owned by PMO)
Service Portfolio Management	• Availability Plan (current investment and future availability needs) • AMIS	• Availability targets • Reports on the status of new/changed Services • Business demands • Service information
Financial Management	• AMIS • Details of any unavailability event • Expenditure justification (design-related – resilience, contract improvements, etc.) • Technical options to meet Service performance • Resources used in managing the AM process • Proposed process budget • Availability Plan • BIA	• Cost of AM • Cost of Service unavailability to justify improvements in Availability Plan (e.g. lost user/IT productivity, lost revenue, overtime, wasted goods and materials, fines/penalties, etc.) • Actuarial costs (e.g. loss of customer goodwill/confidence, damage to reputation, loss of business opportunities) • Cost of providing a required level of availability • Budgeted funds for AM purposes (SD) • BIA

Process (...)	Input from AM to ...	Output from ... to AM
Financial Management cont.		• Cost of Service provision • Cost of Service components • SFA information
Demand Management	• SOA • Projected Service availability • Availability Plan	• PBAs (understand critical Service availability) • UPs • DM techniques
Business Relationship Management	• Agreed requirements/designs • Agreed Service targets • Reports on availability • Prevented incidents (proactive, mitigation due to design, etc.) • SFA report/outcome • Availability accomplishments	• Usage (Availability Plan) • Potential Service targets • Schedules of customer activity (for testing, maintenance, etc.) • PSO agreement • SAC • Customer requirements • Changed requirements • Service review • Forecasts of usage
Service Design		
Design Coordination	• Risk assessment • Availability requirements/designs to be included in the overall Service Designs • Availability Plan	• Policies, guidelines, standards, budgets, models, resources and capabilities • Document templates • Documentation plans • Training plans • Communication/marketing plans • Measurement/metrics plans • Testing plans • Deployment plans • Scheduling • Conflict resolution (resources) • Review, measurement, improvement suggestions • Review of designs ensuring requirements are addressed (utility and warranty) • Requirements
Service Catalogue Management		• Service information
Service Level Management	• BIA • Define/agree realistic Service targets • Availability reports (trend/future requirements; performance) for Service review meetings • Availability Plan • Improvement actions for SIP	• Confirmation of Service availability requirements for a new/changed Service • SIPs • Ensures participation of availability in SLR > SLA negotiations • Service information (monitoring)

Process (...)	Input from AM to ...	Output from ... to AM
Service Level Management cont.	• Input to Cost:Value ratio • Risk assessment • Service Designs to meet recoverability requirements • Service monitoring	• Service requirements and targets • Service reviews • Usage forecasts • Determine/validate Service targets • SFA information
Capacity Management	• Risk assessment • Availability Plan • Unavailability information (if linked to capacity) • Common tools • CFIA, FTA, TOP techniques and information • Resources required to meet availability requirements	• Capacity Plan • Technical resources/information • Service/component functionality reports • Component risk • Input to resilience design • Thresholds/exception reports • SFA information • Common tools • New technologies being considered • Capacity modeling results • Information on new technologies • Performance thresholds • Predictive/forecast reports
IT Service Continuity Management	• BIA • Availability Plan • Ongoing testing schedules • Policy defining the differences between the two processes • Availability requirements for Continuity Plan • Risk assessment and mitigation (countermeasures) information • Completed risk mitigation actions • High-risk Services • Continuity/Availability test results/review and actions • Agreement that availability requirements can be met in the failover environment • Resilience in design to minimize potential invocation of Continuity Plan • Shared costs for CFIA, FTA and other AM techniques	• BIA • Continuity plans, policies, strategies • Continuity designs • Resilience measures • ITSCM Plan test results • SFA information • CFIA, FTA, etc., results (share costs) • Assurance risks are managed • Assurance that predicted risks are managed • Risk assessment and mitigation (countermeasures) information • Completed risk mitigation actions • Data backup and restoration practice
Information Security Management	• Input to formal Corporate Security Policy • Service Designs that include appropriate security controls • Risk assessment and risk management	• Security Policy • Data security policies • Validates designs to ensure appropriate security measures are included • SFA information

Process (…)	Input from AM to …	Output from … to AM
Information Security Management cont.	• Service monitoring information • Security-related Service breaches • Access requests for suppliers or external parties	• Assessment of availability designs for compliance to Security Policy • Risk assessment and risk management
Supplier Management	• Serviceability requirements • Availability Plan for appropriate contract negotiation	• UCs • Serviceability capabilities • Supplier capabilities/resources • Change requirements • SFA information
Service Transition		
Transition Planning and Support	• Risk assessment • Availability Plan • Transition-related process activity results included in updated SDP • Performance targets and measures	
Change Management	• Risk assessment • PSO contributions • Change Schedule • Planned and preventative maintenance schedule • RFC for process improvements • Assessment of RFCs and their impact on availability • RFCs for analysis • RFCs for process improvements • Change design • Testing plan • Remediation plan input	• Change Schedule • PSO • Changes requiring remediation
Service Asset and Configuration Management	• AMIS • Relationships between CIs (resilience) • Availability Plan (as a CI and informational purposes) • BIA results (with ITSCM) • Risk assessment results (with ITSCM, ISM) • Risk reduction measures (with ITSCM, ISM) • Availability activity (CFIA, FTA, SFA, Incident lifecycle analysis, etc.) results	• Relationship information • Technical information (topology, CI relationships) • Relationship information for use in availability/design activities • Basis for CFIA, FTA, identification of Single Points of Failure (SPOFs) and other weaknesses • Details of CIs that need to be risk managed as part of the Availability Plan • License usage/availability • AMIS links
Release and Deployment Management	• Risk assessment • Input to release schedule • Service Designs • Build models/plans	• Release Schedule • Release Plan

Process (...)	Input from AM to ...	Output from ... to AM
Release and Deployment Management cont.	• Test plans • Identification of any availability issue during release planning • Immediate identification of any availability issue during a release	
Service Validation and Testing	• Risk assessment • Tests (resilience, failover, etc.)	• Test results • Validation/verification of SAC
Change Evaluation	• The availability thresholds for Evaluation reports	
Knowledge Management	• Accurate capture, store, use and manage process information and data • New/changed Availability Plan	• Relevant, timely, required and accurate knowledge, information and data
Service Operation		
Event Management	• Availability thresholds for defining monitoring for events • Operational procedures for recognizing, logging, escalating, communicating events • Defines event significance and thresholds	• Events indicating a potential breach of SLA/OLA requirement • Threshold/exception reports
Incident Management	• Expectations/thresholds for availability of Services for identification of incidents • Assist with resolution of any availability-related incident • Reduce gaps in Expanded Incident Lifecycle • Diagnostic scripts	• Availably-related incident information • Unavailability information • Availability data • SFA information
Request Fulfillment	• Input to RF workflow designs	• RF issues related to availability (track via IM)
Problem Management	• Availability Plan • Assist with resolution of any availability-related problem • Shared tools/techniques (CFIA, FTA, SFA, etc.)	• Problem data • Proactive reporting of potential threats to availability • Root cause analysis • Improvement suggestions • SFA information • Shared tools/techniques (CFIA, FTA, SFA, etc.) • Methods to reduce downtime
Access Management	• Methods for granting/revoking rights	• Reports on rights granted/revoked

Process (...)	Input from AM to ...	Output from ... to AM
Continual Service Improvement		
7-step Improvement Process	• Proactive service/component availability opportunities • Process improvement opportunities • Specific Service improvements based on AM events	• CSI Register • Updated Availability Plan • Recommendations for improvement implantation plans

Function (...)	Input from AM to ...	Output from ... to AM
Service Desk	• Resolved availability-related incidents	• Complaints • Availability-related incidents
Technical Management	• Request for technical knowledge and skills in planning and design activities	• Technical expertise to assist or complete new/changed Service Design • Maintenance schedules/activities • Participation within process activities (CFIA, SFA, FTA, TO) • Investigation of poor service performance (major problem review, SIP)
Application Management	• Request for technical knowledge and skills in planning and design activities	• Technical expertise to assist or complete new/changed Service Design • Maintenance schedules/activities • Participation within process activities (CFIA, SFA, FTA, TO) • Investigation of poor service performance (major problem review, SIP)
IT Operations Management	• Monitoring criteria	

Capacity Management (CapM)

Purpose

"Right amount, right time, cost-justified" – ensuring sufficient resources/capacity are available to meet the current and future agreed requirements cost-effectively.

Objectives

- Produce and maintain a Capacity Plan.
- Provide guidance on all capacity-related matters (e.g. incidents, problems, etc.).
- Manage service and component capacity to ensure agreed service targets are met.
- Assess RFCs for impact to the Capacity Plan and current service delivery.
- Proactive cost-justified capacity improvements.

Process (...)	Input from CapM to ...	Output from ... to CapM
Service Strategy		
Strategy Management for IT Services	• Capacity Plan • Proactive CapM measures • BCM and SCM activities supporting and enhancing organizational Strategy	• Mission/vision • Service Strategy • Policies • Strategy requirements for new/changed Services • Project Portfolio (owned by PMO)
Service Portfolio Management	• Capacity Plan (current investment and future capacity needs) • CMIS	• Reports on the status of new/changed Services • Business plans/requirements • Service Portfolio
Financial Management	• CMIS (e.g. usage and performance data, etc.) • Resource details to support accounting or charging • Technical options to meet Service performance • Cost allocation methods based on resource usage • Details of predicted PBAs/UPs • Upgrade predictions to support budgeting • Use Moore's Law and Parkinson's Law of Data to support resource procurement • Proposed process budget • Capacity Plan • Predictive/forecast reports • Details to support charging of a new requirement • Cost allocation mechanics based upon resource usage	• Cost of CapM • Process budget • Assistance in costing Capacity options • Budgeted funds for CapM purposes – Capacity Plan • Financial plans/budgets within BCM and CapM as a unit must coincide with FM practices • Current budget/cost effectiveness • Costs (Service provision, CIs, etc.)

Process (...)	Input from CapM to ...	Output from ... to CapM
Demand Management	• Policies for management of demand when resources are over-utilized • How to match supply/demand in design and operation of the Service • DM techniques/restrictions • PBAs/UPs (performance, utilization, throughput)	• Policies for management of demand when resources are over-utilized • How to match supply/demand in design and operation of the Service • DM techniques/restrictions • PBAs/UPS (performance, utilization, throughput)
Business Relationship Management	• Reports on capacity (workload, usage, forecasts, etc.)	• Projected Service usage/consumption (Capacity Plan)
Service Design		
Design Coordination	• Capacity requirements/designs to be included in the SDP	• Policies, guidelines, standards, budgets, models, resources and capabilities • Document templates • Documentation plans • Training plans • Communication/marketing plans • Measurement/metrics plans • Testing plans • Deployment plans • Scheduling • Conflict resolution (resources) • Review, measurement, improvement suggestions • Review of designs ensuring requirements are addressed (utility and warranty)
Service Catalogue Management		

Service Level Management	• Capacity Plan
	• Define/agree realistic Service targets
	• Identification of throughput and peaks and troughs for SLAs Reports for Service review meetings
	  o Trend/usage
	  o Resource (technology, human, etc.) limitations
	  o Identify data for SLA reviews (batch jobs, response times, etc.)
	  o Service-based reports
	  o Exception reports
		• SIPs
		• BCM information
		• SCM information
		• Assists in identifying and predicting the behavior of the business drivers of capacity
		• Details of Services to be considered if DM invoked
		• Capacity target validation
		• Capacity-related Service breach data

Availability Management	• Capacity Plan • Technical resources/information	• Risk assessment • Availability Plan

Process (…)	Input from CapM to …	Output from … to CapM
Availability Management cont.	• Service/component functionality reports • Component risk • Input to resilience design • Thresholds/exception reports • SFA information • Common tools • New technologies being considered • Capacity modeling results • Information on new technologies • Performance thresholds • Predictive/forecast reports	• Unavailability information (if linked to capacity) • Common tools • CFIA, FTA, TO techniques and information • Resources required to meet availability requirements
IT Service Continuity Management	• Capacity Plan (including ITSCM requirements) • Input to BIA and risk activities • Confirm capacity required for risk reduction measures • Exception reports • Participation in Continuity testing • Assist in assessing recovery options • Available resources for the Continuity environment • Infrastructure needed to provide minimum requirements (performance/throughput) • Assist in evaluation of possible recovery options • Component/service monitor/analyze/tune information for use in failover environment	• Continuity plans, policies, strategies • Resources required to meet Continuity requirements • Information for Capacity Plan (design and resource needs)
Information Security Management	• Security-based thresholds, events, alerts, warnings • Service monitoring information • Service breaches • Ensure that situations of under-/over-capacity do not pose security risks • Ensures capacity configurations take into account potential multi-layer security protocols	• Security controls • Assessment of potential or new technologies for security implications
Supplier Management	• Capacity-related input to supplier contract definition, negotiation and agreement • New/changed capacity requirements • Technological innovation	• "On demand" contract conditions based on Capacity Plan/DM techniques • Technical performance details of contracted CIs • Technological innovation

Process (...)	Input from CapM to ...	Output from ... to CapM
Service Transition		
Transition Planning and Support	• Transition-related process activity results included in updated SDP	
Change Management	• RFC impact assessment on current capacity • RFC for capacity improvements • Remediation plan input • RFC for process improvements	• Change Schedule • RFC for CapM assessment • Remediated changes
Service Asset and Configuration Management	• CMIS • Capacity Plan as a document CI • Performance information may be a CI attribute	• CMS/CMDB • Technical topology/architectures • Identification of potential bottlenecks or other points of weakness • Knowledge of the relationships between Service elements could be important if there are capacity problems • CMIS links
Release and Deployment Management	• Service Designs • Build models/plans • Identification of any capacity issue during release planning • Immediate identification of any capacity issue during a release	• Release Plans • Information to update Capacity Plan
Service Validation and Testing	• Capacity-related input to testing requirements and planning (e.g. software licensing, Service staffing requirements, etc.)	• Confirmation of capacity requirement fulfillment during validation/testing activities
Change Evaluation	• The capacity thresholds for Evaluation reports	•
Knowledge Management	• Accurate capture, store, use and manage process information and data • New/changed Capacity Plan	• Relevant, timely, required and accurate knowledge, information and data
Service Operation		
Event Management	• Basis for alarms, alerts, thresholds to be included in monitoring • Event correlation tables, rules, responses • Operational procedures for recognizing, logging, escalating, communicating events • Defines event significance and thresholds	• Events indicating a potential breach of SLA/OLA requirement

Process (...)	Input from CapM to ...	Output from ... to CapM
Incident Management	• Expectations/thresholds for capacity of Services for identification of incidents • Assistance in resolution of capacity-related incidents • Advice on workarounds • Diagnostic scripts	• Capacity-related incident information
Request Fulfillment		
Problem Management	• Assistance in resolution of capacity-related problems • Provides resource for problem resolution team • Highlights potential capacity problem	• Capacity-related problem information
Access Management		
Continual Service Improvement		
7-step Improvement Process	• Process improvement opportunities • Specific Service improvements based on CapM event • Risk assessment and mitigation plans • Capacity Plan • Trend analysis • Monitored data • New technology impact • Assist in defining monitoring and data collection capabilities • Accountable for infrastructure monitoring and data collection • Ensure proper tools are in place for data gathering • Trend information on service/component use and analysis of data from a historical perspective • Assess component performance against technical specification • Input to improvement prioritization • Identify improvement opportunities	• CSI Register • Process improvement opportunities • Updated Capacity Plan • Monitoring procedures/plan • Recommendations for improvement implantation plans

Function (…)	Input from CapM to …	Output from … to CapM
Service Desk	• Resolved capacity-related incidents	• Escalated capacity-related incidents
Technical Management	• Request of technical expertise	• Technical performance details (trending) • Participate in modeling exercises • Manage/store capacity-related performance data
Application Management	• Request of technical expertise	• Application performance details (trending) • Participate in application sizing exercises
IT Operations Management	• Monitoring criteria	• Backup/restoration of CMIS

IT Service Continuity Management (ITSCM)

Purpose

Support Business Continuity Plans by managing risks (i.e. risk reduction; recovery of IT Services) in order to always provide the agreed minimal level of Service.

Objectives

- Produce and maintain Continuity Plans reflecting agreed performance parameters.
- Complete and maintain accurate and up-to-date BIA information (AM, ISM).
- Complete and maintain accurate and up-to-date risk information; manage risk within the agreed and stated risk tolerance levels of the business (AM, ISM).
- Provide advice/guidance on all continuity-related issues.
- Ensure appropriate and agreed continuity measures are in place.
- Assess the impact of all changes to the Continuity Plans.
- Ensure cost-justifiable proactive availability methods are deployed.
- Ensure third party contracts/agreements provide the necessary resources to support the agreed Continuity parameters (SuppM).

Process (…)	Input from ITSCM to …	Output from … to ITSCM
Service Strategy		
Strategy Management for IT Services	• ITSCM policy which meets mission/vision • Continuity plans/measures in place to meet Service Strategy • Risk assessment and countermeasures • Review of strategy/plans from a Continuity perspective	• Mission/vision • Service Strategy • Policies • Business Strategy, plans, risk tolerance • Strategy requirements for new/changed Services • Project Portfolio (owned by PMO) • Provides definition of "disaster"
Service Portfolio Management	• Continuity Plan (current countermeasures and recovery plans for each Service) • BIA (risks) • Capabilities for Continuity actions	• Services that must be considered for Continuity planning, as agreed • Recovery criteria • Risk information • New/changed Services • Service Portfolio • Service Catalogue • Customer Portfolio • Customer Agreement Portfolio
Financial Management	• Continuity Plans (for costing and billing apportionment) • Resources used in managing the ITSCM process • Proposed process budget	• Cost of ITSCM • Budgeted funds for ITSCM purposes • Evaluation of recovery and Continuity options (costs) • Ensures third party suppliers are paid

Process (...)	Input from ITSCM to ...	Output from ... to ITSCM
Financial Management cont.		• Current and future financial plans and strategies • Budgets (ensuring funds for Continuity activities) • Service costs • Apportionment/charging of Services to include Continuity costs
Demand Management	• BIA	• PBAs/UPs • Sizing recovery options
Business Relationship Management	• Communicate change in risk or impact to business processes • ITSCM Plans • ITSCM testing schedule (for customer involvement) • BIA outcome • ITSCM test reports	• BCP requirements • Provides definition of "disaster" (customer view) • Service priorities/criticality • Assurance of business awareness of Continuity Plans/measures • Discussion of Continuity planning with customers • Validation of Continuity measure are valid for current environment • Recovery criteria
Service Design		
Design Coordination	• Continuity requirements/designs to be included in the SDP	• Policies, guidelines, standards, budgets, models, resources and capabilities • Document templates • Documentation plans • Training plans • Communication/marketing plans • Measurement/metrics plans • Testing plans • Deployment plans • Scheduling • Conflict resolution (resources) • Review, measurement, improvement suggestions • Review of designs ensuring requirements are addressed (utility and warranty) • Designs/plans for new/changed Services for review/agreement
Service Catalogue Management	• Continuity information to be included in the Service description	• Service Catalogue
Service Level Management	• BIA • Define/agree realistic Service targets/levels during Continuity event	• SLRs and SLAs in DR situations • Details of all "standard" SLA requirements • Service priorities to check against customer view

Process (...)	Input from ITSCM to ...	Output from ... to ITSCM
Service Level Management cont.	• Capabilities for Continuity actions • Risk assessment • Continuity Plan (for reference within SLAs) with confirmed actions	• Agreed levels of Service to be provided in a disaster • Review of tests • Assurance of business awareness • Assurance that OLAs/UCs include support required for ITSCM • New/changed Service targets • SLAs (Continuity targets and standard details) • Service priorities/criticality • Test result review (meets agreed parameters) • Assurance of customer awareness of responsibilities and IT measures/activities • Agreed Continuity testing timetables (SLAs) • Monitor/review/report on Service targets after invocation of the Continuity Plan
Availability Management	• BIA • Continuity plans, policies, strategies • Continuity designs • Resilience measures • Continuity Plan test results • SFA information • CFIA, FTA, etc. results (share costs) • Assurance risks are managed • Assurance that predicted risks are managed • Risk assessment and mitigation (countermeasures) information • Completed risk mitigation actions • Data backup and restoration practice	• BIA • Availability Plan • Ongoing testing schedules • Policy defining the differences between the two processes • Availability requirements for Continuity Plan • Risk assessment and mitigation (countermeasures) information • Completed risk mitigation actions • High-risk Services • Continuity/Availability test results/review and actions • Agreement that availability requirements can be met in the failover environment • Resilience in design to minimize potential invocation of Continuity Plan • Shared costs for CFIA, FTA and other AM techniques
Capacity Management	• Continuity plans, policies, strategies • Resources required to meet Continuity requirements • Information for Capacity Plan (design and resource needs)	• Capacity Plan (including ITSCM requirements) • Input to BIA and risk activities • Confirm capacity required for risk reduction measures • Exception reports • Participation in Continuity testing

Process (...)	Input from ITSCM to ...	Output from ... to ITSCM
Capacity Management cont.		• Assist in assessing recovery options • Available resources for the Continuity environment • Infrastructure needed to provide minimum requirements (performance/throughput) • Assist in evaluation of possible recovery options • Component/service monitor/analyze/tune information for use in failover environment
Information Security Management	• Continuity plans (requirement of ISO/IEC 20000), policies, strategies • Risk assessment and mitigation information • Completed risk mitigation actions • BIA • Invocation of the Continuity Plan parameters • Assurance the Continuity Plan adequately protects Service CIs during a disaster • Assurance data/information protected during a continuity event	• Risk assessment and mitigation information • Assessment of Continuity measures for compliance to Security Policy • Ensure mitigation/recovery methods do not adversely impact Security Policy requirements • Oversight/review of ITSCM tests ensuring security of data/information during tests or invocation • Assurance that security failures will not compound a disaster situation • Completed risk mitigation actions • BIA • Parameters/information on major security event (invoke the Continuity Plan) • Security requirements to be followed in a Continuity event
Supplier Management	• Requirements (terms/conditions) for Continuity-based suppliers • Negotiation skills • Requirements for third party testing and participation in on-site testing	• SCMIS • Contracts support Continuity requirements and plans • Supplier Policy • Management of Continuity-based suppliers
Service Transition		
Transition Planning and Support	• Transition-related process activity results included in updated SDP • Inclusion of TPS-related activities, areas, functionality within the Continuity Plan, if appropriate	• Assist, as needed, during the invocation of the Continuity Plan

Process (...)	Input from ITSCM to ...	Output from ... to ITSCM
Change Management	• Assessed RFCs (impact to Continuity Plan) • CAB member, if necessary • ITSCM testing schedule • RFC for process improvements • RFC to update Continuity Plan based on approved changes • RFCs to improve process/continuity measures	• RFCs (assess for impact to Continuity Plan) • Change Schedule • Approval to update Continuity Plan
Service Asset and Configuration Management	• ITSCM configuration baseline • Continuity Plan (document CI)	• CMS/CMDB • Continuity baseline • Critical components/services to be included in Continuity Plan • Configuration details of alternate/failover services/environments • Full version control details of the ITSCM Plan • Configuration details of alternative Services to be used in a disaster • Up-to-date information about the content of the infrastructure
Release and Deployment Management	• Identification of Continuity issues (Release Plan) • Continuity Plan • Immediate identification of any Continuity issue during a release	• Plans for deploying Services into the failover environment (post invocation of the Continuity Plan) • Tested Continuity Plans
Service Validation and Testing	• Testing requirements/parameters • ITSCM testing schedule • ITSCM test scenarios	• Test results
Change Evaluation	• Continuity Plans • Continuity test plans/results	• Assessment of Continuity Plans as per Service Designs
Knowledge Management	• Post-testing/invocation information and lessons learned • Accurate capture, store, use and manage process information and data • New/changed Continuity Plan	• Past test results • Test information • Test scenarios • Information that may impact tests or invocation of Continuity Plan • Relevant, timely, required and accurate knowledge, information and data (SKMS)

Process (...)	Input from ITSCM to ...	Output from ... to ITSCM
Service Operation		
Event Management	• Thresholds for critical (fragile) components (proactive prevention)	• Communication of an event
Incident Management	• Invocation of the Continuity Plan parameters	• Parameters/information on major incident (invoke the Continuity Plan) • Incidents that may invoke the Continuity Plan • Incidents caused during/after invocation of the Continuity Plan (effectiveness of Continuity Plan)
Request Fulfillment		
Problem Management	• Invocation of the Continuity Plan parameters • Resource for problem-solving team	• Parameters/information on major problem (invoke the Continuity Plan) • High-risk problems that may threaten Service continuity • Assistance in understanding the "why" of a failed deployment of the Continuity Plan • Assistance in resolving a failed deployment of the Continuity Plan • Proactive PM methods to avoid a potential disaster
Access Management	• Overall security standards within which AcM must perform • Authorization (with AM) policies for granting data/information/Service access	• Reports of access granted • Access requests for suppliers or external parties • Assurance access controls effective/active in failover environment
Continual Service Improvement		
7-step Improvement Process	• Risk assessment and mitigation plans • ITSCM Plan • Identify improvement opportunities based on ITSCM events	• Updated ITSCM Plan • Process improvement opportunities • Recommendations for improvement implantation plans

Function (...)	Input from ITSCM to ...	Output from ... to ITSCM
Service Desk	• Information to communicate, in a Continuity situation • Disaster definition and what will trigger its execution • Continuity Plans	• Escalated events • Incidents related to failover environment
Technical Management	• Continuity Plans	• Participation in testing Continuity Plans (system, service, full/partial plan, third party, etc. • Participate in coordination/recovery team • Participate in training/awareness activities • Participation in maintenance of plans • Risk assessment • Execute any risk mitigation activities (countermeasures, resilience, etc.) • Participate in writing recovery plans
Application Management	• Continuity Plans	• Participation in testing Continuity Plans (system, service, full/partial plan, third party, etc. • Participate in coordination/recovery team • Participate in training/awareness activities
IT Operations Management	• Continuity Plans	• Participation in testing Continuity Plans (system, service, full/ partial plan, third party, etc • Participate in coordination/recovery team • Participation in maintenance of plans • Participate in training/awareness activities

Information Security Management (ISM)

Purpose

Ensure the confidentiality, integrity, and availability (accessibility) of organizational assets, information, data, and IT Services meets the agreed business requirements (cost-effectively), now and in the future.

Objectives

- Protect the interests of those relying on information (including the systems that deliver the information).
- Confidentiality (only those authorized access/use of the information).
- Integrity (information is accurate and consistent over its lifespan).
- Availability/accessibility (information is usable when required).
- Authenticity and non-repudiation (data/information transaction can be trusted).

Process (...)	Input from ISM to ...	Output from ... to ISM
Service Strategy		
Strategy Management for IT Services	• ISM policy meeting mission/vision • Security controls to enhance achievement of Service Strategy • Reports on security breaches	• Mission/vision • Service Strategy • Policies • Strategy requirements for new/changed Services • Project Portfolio (owned by PMO) • Business Strategy policies/plans • Business Plans (current/future) • Risks • Change to corporate governance • Business security policy • Corporate risk management • Review/revision of IT Strategy plans, policies
Service Portfolio Management	• Security checks on access to Service Portfolio • Security controls • SMIS	• Service Portfolio • New/changed Services • Service information • Strategic risks • Service models
Financial Management	• SMIS • Resources used in managing the ISM process • Proposed process budget • Process activities • Security controls protecting financial data/information	• Cost of ISM • Input to business case for new/changed security measures • Financial options on security options

Process (...)	Input from ISM to ...	Output from ... to ISM
Demand Management	• Results of security assessment on mitigation techniques • Security Policy	• Current mitigation techniques to ensure no breach in security protocols • UPs
Business Relationship Management	• Change in risk or mitigation methods (communicate to Customer) • Reports on security (breaches, controls, etc.)	• Security requirements • Business plans (current/future) • Legislative/regulatory requirements • Business needs
Service Design		
Design Coordination	• Information security requirements / designs to be included in the SDP • Security Policy (ensure all designs conform to its requirements)	• Policies, guidelines, standards, budgets, models, resources and capabilities • Document templates • Documentation plans • Training plans • Communication/marketing plans • Measurement/metrics plans • Testing plans • Deployment plans • Scheduling • Conflict resolution (resources) • Review, measurement, improvement suggestions • Review of designs ensuring requirements are addressed (utility and warranty)
Service Catalogue Management	• Security information for Service description	• Service Catalogue
Service Level Management	• Assist in security requirement negotiations • Define/agree realistic Service targets	• Security requirements • Service information • Service monitoring information • Service breaches • Investigation/reporting on security events
Availability Management	• Security Policy • Data security policies • Validates designs to ensure appropriate security measures are included • SFA information • Assessment of availability designs for compliance to Security Policy • Risk assessment and risk management	• Input to formal Corporate Security Policy • Service Designs that include appropriate security controls • Risk assessment and risk management • Service monitoring information • Security-related Service breaches • Access requests for suppliers or external parties

Process (...)	Input from ISM to ...	Output from ... to ISM
Capacity Management	• Security controls • Assessment of potential or new technologies for security implications	• Security-based thresholds, events, alerts, warnings • Service monitoring information • Service breaches • Ensure that situations of under-/over-capacity do not pose security risks • Ensures capacity configurations take into account potential multi-layer security protocols
IT Service Continuity Management	• Risk assessment and mitigation information • Assessment of Continuity measures for compliance to Security Policy • Ensure mitigation/recovery methods do not adversely impact Security Policy requirements • Oversight/review of ITSCM tests ensuring security of data/information during tests or invocation • Assurance that security failures will not compound a disaster situation • Completed risk mitigation actions • BIA • Parameters/information on major security event (invoke the Continuity Plan) • Security requirements to be followed in a Continuity event	• Continuity plans (requirement of ISO/IEC 20000), policies, strategies • Risk assessment and mitigation information • Completed risk mitigation actions • BIA • Invocation of the Continuity Plan parameters • Assurance the Continuity Plan adequately protest Service CIs during a disaster • Assurance data/information protected during a Continuity event
Supplier Management	• Security controls for all suppliers (access and/or interface with data/information) • Specific security-related terms and conditions for contracts detailing third party responsibilities • New/changed security requirements	• Conformity measures • Access requests for suppliers or external parties • Contracts for review to ensure conformance to Security Policy
Service Transition		
Transition Planning and Support	• Transition-related process activity results included in updated SDP	
Change Management	• Member of the CAB/ECAB (potential) • Assessment of RFCs for impact on Security Policies	• Authorized changes that have been security assessed • Risk assessment and risk management

Process (...)	Input from ISM to ...	Output from ... to ISM
Change Management cont.	• RFCs for process improvements, improved security controls, etc. • Information on unauthorized changes from security breaches	• Change Schedule
Service Asset and Configuration Management	• SMIS links • Information on access to CI records • Security controls • Security Policy • Supporting ISM-based policies (access, password, email, internet, anti-virus, etc.) • Access control information (AM) • Security checks/tests to ensure proper access to CMDB/CMS is attained/followed • Security checks on access to the Definitive Medial Library (DML)	• CMS/CMDB • Relationships between Service components from a ISM view
Release and Deployment Management	• Define the secure handling of CIs as per the Security Policy within the Release Policy • Confirmation that release package meets necessary security standards as per Security Policy	• Release Policy • Release Plans (confirmation of security measures to protect release of CIs)
Service Validation and Testing	• Security policies around test data • Security Policy as applied to test environment	• Reports on security-related testing
Change Evaluation		
Knowledge Management	• Security check on access to SKMS/CMS/CMDB • Accurate capture, store, use and manage process information and data • New/changed Security controls/policies	• Relevant, timely, required and accurate knowledge, information and data
Service Operation		
Event Management	• Critical business applications and/or business processes for monitoring • Thresholds for critical (fragile) components (proactive prevention) • Security-based thresholds, events, alerts, warnings	• Reports on security-based thresholds, events, alerts, warnings

Process (...)	Input from ISM to ...	Output from ... to ISM
Incident Management	• Definition of "security incident" • Manages all security-related incidents	• Security incident escalation • Security incident details
Request Fulfillment	• ISM policies and requirements related to Service Requests	
Problem Management	• Provides resource for Problem Resolution team, as needed	• Root cause and possible resolution of security-related events • Security problem details
Access Management	• Overall security standards within which AcM must perform • Authorization (with AM) policies for granting data, information, Service access	• Recommended updates to the overall Security Management Strategy • Reports of access granted/changed/revoked • Access requests for suppliers or external parties • Assurance access controls effective/active in failover environment
Continual Service Improvement		
7-step Improvement Process	• Specific Service improvements based on ISM events • Risk assessment and mitigation plans • Define monitoring for security based on organizational security policies • Collect data around CIA of data/information • Trend analysis of security breaches • Document/assess security-related incidents for trends and cause • Validate success of risk mitigation efforts • Identify improvement opportunities	• Communication of improvement initiatives • Recommendations for improvement implantation plans

Function (...)	Input from ISM to ...	Output from ... to ISM
Service Desk	• Definition of a security incident • Escalation paths	• Escalated security incident
Technical Management	• Security Policy • Training/awareness	• Activity execution within Security Policy/controls • Policing/reporting • Technical assistance with security events (forensic information/evidence) • Operational security control (assign privileged access, monitor and control access, remove when not needed) • Screening/vetting • Documented policies/procedures that include relevant security controls as dictated by the Security Policy
Application Management	• Security Policy	• Activity execution within Security Policy/controls • Policing/reporting • Technical assistance with security events (forensic information/evidence) • Operational security control (assign privileged access, monitor and control access, remove when not needed) • Screening/vetting • Documented policies/procedures that include relevant security controls as dictated by the Security Policy
IT Operations Management	• Security Policy	• Activity execution within Security Policy/controls • Policing/reporting • Technical assistance with security events (forensic information/evidence) • Operational security control • Screening/vetting • Documented policies/procedures that include relevant security controls as dictated by the Security Policy

Supplier Management (SuppM)

Purpose

Obtain "value for money" from suppliers via appropriate contracts and provide seamless Service quality.

Objectives

- Manage supplier relationships.
- Ensure contracts aligned with business need (SLM).
- Obtain value for money from contracts/suppliers.
- Manage supplier performance.
- Negotiate/agree contacts and manage them through their lifecycle (SLM, ITSCM).
- Create/manage/maintain a SCMIS.

Process (...)	Input from SuppM to ...	Output from ... to SuppM
Service Strategy		
Strategy Management for IT Services	• Supplier/contract performance reports (to meet Strategy)	• Mission/vision • Service Strategy • Policies • Strategy requirements for new/changed Services • New/changed corporate governance • New/changed IT governance
Service Portfolio Management	• SCMIS • Supplier/contract performance report • At risk suppliers/contract • Links between suppliers and Services provided (SCMIS/CMDB/CMS/SKMS)	• New/changed Services • Service Portfolio • Project Portfolio • Customer Portfolio • Customer Agreement Portfolio • Application Portfolio
Financial Management	• SCMIS • Resources used in managing the SuppM process • Proposed process budget • Supplier contract performance data	• Cost of SuppM • UC cost • Financial penalties or incentives • Policies for contract management • Legislative, regulatory, organizational constraints for contract negotiations and actions • Reports on payments to suppliers • Current IT budgets (overall, by process, by department, by service, etc.) • Standard terms/conditions for payments, etc. • Guidance on purchase and procurement matters

Process (...)	Input from SuppM to ...	Output from ... to SuppM
Demand Management	• "On demand" contract conditions based on Capacity Plan/DM techniques	• PBAs/UPs
Business Relationship Management	• UCs	• Service requirements • Complaints/compliments • New/changed business needs • Satisfaction survey results
Service Design		
Design Coordination	• Supplier risk assessment • Shared and agreed practices to support process activities and the overall Service Design • Supplier and/or contract information pertinent to Service Design activities	• Shared and agreed practices to support process activities and the overall Service Design • Information pertinent to contract review to support design activities • New/changed designs
Service Catalogue Management		• Service Catalogue
Service Level Management	• UCs • Policy for shared activities • Contract performance • Contract changes • Manage complaints/compliments • Supplier Policy • Supplier performance information (potentially)	• SLR for contract negotiations • Policy for shared activities • Manage complaints/compliments • New/changed Service requirements • Negotiation assistance • Definition of Service targets • Investigation of SLA/SLR breaches on account of poor supplier performance • Information for SuppM review process • Assistance in contract management, if necessary
Availability Management	• UCs • Serviceability capabilities • Supplier capabilities/resources • Change requirements • SFA information	• Serviceability requirements • Availability Plan for appropriate contract negotiation
Capacity Management	• "On demand" contract conditions based on Capacity Plan/DM techniques • Technical performance details of contracted CIs • Technological innovation	• Capacity-related input to supplier contract definition, negotiation and agreement • New/changed capacity requirements • Technological innovation
IT Service Continuity Management	• SCMIS • Contracts support Continuity requirements and plans • Supplier Policy • Management of Continuity-based suppliers	• Requirements (terms/conditions) for Continuity-based suppliers • Negotiation skills • Requirements for third party testing and participation in on-site testing

Process (...)	Input from SuppM to ...	Output from ... to SuppM
Information Security Management	• Conformity measures • Access requests for suppliers or external parties • Contracts for review to ensure conformance to Security Policy	• Security controls for all suppliers (access and/or interface with data/information) • Specific security-related terms and conditions for contracts detailing third party responsibilities • New/changed security requirements
Service Transition		
Transition Planning and Support	• Terms/conditions of supplier contracts allowing good Transition planning	• Requirements for necessary CIs in the transition of a new/changed Service
Change Management	• CAB member (if necessary) • Review of RFCs for impact to contracts • RFC for changed contracts/agreements • Verification of procured components to approved RFC • RFC for process improvement	• Terms/conditions to assist in scheduling (e.g. procurement times) • Approved RFCs • Change Schedule
Service Asset and Configuration Management	• SCMIS • Warranty information • POC for supplier • Contract details • Supplier details • Information on new CIs • Other CI attributes	• CMS/CMDB
Release and Deployment Management	• Terms/conditions for suppliers allowing good Release planning • Participation in Deployment, as contracted	• Requirements for CI delivery • Information to update UCs
Service Validation and Testing		• Test results of third party assets
Change Evaluation		
Knowledge Management	• SCMIS • Supplier knowledgebase • Accurate capture, store, use and manage process information and data • Delivery of user information	• SCMIS (relationship information; contact details, etc.) • Relevant, timely, required and accurate knowledge, information and data
Service Operation		
Event Management		
Incident Management	• Supplier-related information in support of incident diagnosis/workarounds	• Incidents related to a specific supplier

Process (...)	Input from SuppM to ...	Output from ... to SuppM
Incident Management cont.	• What Services the provider supports/provides for assigning incidents	• Incident diagnosis/workarounds • Satisfaction survey results
Request Fulfillment	• If outsourced, contract details for RF workflow designs	• If the process activities are outsourced, details of a SuppM-related request event
Problem Management	• Provides resource for Problem Resolution team • Supplier-related KE information incorporated into organizational knowledgebase	• Details of a SuppM-related problem • Investigation of SLA/SLR breaches on account of poor Supplier performance
Access Management	• Requirements for third party access to Services, CIs, data, etc.	• Reports on Supplier access provided (rejected)
Continual Service Improvement		
7-step Improvement Process	• UCs • Identify improvement opportunities • Specific Service improvements based on SuppM events	• Process improvement opportunities • CSI Register • Communication of improvement initiatives • Recommendations for improvement implantation plans

Function (...)	Input from SuppM to ...	Output from ... to SuppM
Service Desk		
Technical Management		• Manage suppliers/contracts for specific CIs, if necessary
Application Management		
IT Operations Management		

Service Transition (ST)

Purpose

Ensure that new/changed Services meet business needs as defined in Service Strategy and Service Design.

Objectives

- Efficient/effective, risk-mitigated Service Changes.
- Minimally invasive, risk-mitigated Service Deployment.
- Ensure changes meet expected value, and, when they do not, level-set customer expectations.
- Capture, maintain and deliver required knowledge and information about Services and associated CIs/assets.

Lifecycle Phase (...)	Input from ST to ...	Output from ... to ST
Service Strategy	• Transitioned Services • Information and feedback for business cases and Service Portfolio • Response to change proposals • Service Portfolio updates • Change Schedule • Feedback on strategies and policies • Financial information for input to budgets • Financial reports • Knowledge and information in the SKMS	• Vision and mission • Service Portfolio • Policies • Strategies and strategic plans • Priorities • Change proposals, including utility and warranty requirements and expected timescales • Financial information and budgets • Input to Change evaluation and CAB meetings

Service Design	• Service Catalogue updates
	• Feedback on all aspects of SD and SDPs
	• Input and feedback on Transition plans
	• Response to RFCs
	• Knowledge and information in the SKMS (including the CMS)
	• Design errors identified in Transition for re-design
	• Evaluation reports
		• Service Catalogue
		• SDPs, including:
		  o Details of utility and warranty
		  o Acceptance criteria
		  o Service models
		  o Designs and interface specifications
		  o Transition plans
		  o Operation plans and procedures
		• RFCs to transition or deploy new or changed Services
		• Input to Change evaluation and CAB meetings
		• Designs for Service Transition processes and procedures
		• SLAs, OLAs, UCs

Lifecycle Phase (...)	Input from ST to ...	Output from ... to ST
Service Operation	• New or changed Services • Known errors • Standard changes for use in RF • Knowledge and information in the SKMS (including the CMS) • Change Schedule	• RFCs to resolve operational issues • Feedback on quality of Transition activities • Input to operational testing • Actual performance information • Input to Change evaluation and CAB meetings
Continual Service Improvement	• Test reports • ChE reports • Knowledge and information in the SKMS • Achievements against metrics, KPIs and CSFs • Improvement opportunities logged in the CSI Register	• Results of customer and user satisfaction surveys • Input to testing requirements • Data required for metrics, KPIs, CSFs • Input to ChE and CAB meetings • Service reports • RFCs for implementing improvements

From: *ITIL® Service Transition*, Table 3.1. ©Crown copyright 2011. Reproduced under license from the Cabinet Office.

Transition Planning and Support (TPS)

Purpose

Provide overall planning and resource coordination for Transition activities.

Objectives

- Ensure appropriate resources are used (available) ensuring agreed requirements are met.
- Coordinate activities across all resources and groups preventing resource/time conflicts.
- Ensure new/changed Service is deployed within established cost, time, and quality.
- Ensure appropriate tools, management systems, processes, measurement systems, and architectures meet design requirements.
- Ensure standardized and common work techniques (efficiency and effectiveness within activities).
- Ensure plans are clearly defined and properly communicated/coordinated between all projects/groups.
- Mitigate and communicate risks.
- Monitor and improve the Transition activities.

Process (...)	Input from TPS to ...	Output from ... to TPS
Service Strategy		
Strategy Management for IT Services	• Actions and plans for cultural, organizational and Service Changes to meet strategic plans • Transition policies	• Mission/vision • Service Strategy (underpins Transition policies) • Policies • Input to Service Transition protocols
Service Portfolio Management	• Transition updates	• Service Portfolio and supporting portfolios for a full picture of Service delivery and customers • Submission of change proposals
Financial Management	• Proposed process budget • Budget/resources for Transition activities • Activity details for Service cost calculations	• Cost of TPS
Demand Management		• Long-term information around resource requirements
Business Relationship Management	• Transition plans • Communication Plan • Requests for customer resources for Transition activities (e.g. testing, evaluation, pilot, etc.)	• Customer response from Communication Plan • Service requirements

Process (...)	Input from TPS to ...	Output from ... to TPS
Service Design		
Design Coordination	• Shared and agreed practices to ensure a smooth transfer between design and transition activities	• Complete SDP (Service charter, Service specifications, Service models, architectural design, definition/design of each associated release with associated entry/exit criteria, assembly Service components for the release package, RDM plans, SAC, etc.) • Shared and agreed practices to ensure a smooth transfer between design and transition activities
Service Catalogue Management	• Communication Plan (adding new/changed Service to Catalogue)	
Service Level Management	• Communication Plan	• SLRs/SLAs • Transition-related process activity results included in updated SDP
Availability Management		• Risk assessment • Availability Plan • Transition-related process activity results included in updated SDP • Performance targets and measures
Capacity Management		• Transition-related process activity results included in updated SDP • Performance targets and measures
IT Service Continuity Management	• Assist, as needed, during the invocation of the Continuity Plan	• Transition-related process activity results included in updated SDP • Inclusion of TPS-related activities, areas, functionality within the Continuity Plan, if appropriate
Information Security Management		• Transition-related process activity results included in updated SDP
Supplier Management	• Requirements for necessary CIs in the transition of a new/changed Service	• Terms/conditions of supplier contracts allowing good transition planning
Service Transition		
Change Management	• Communication Plan	• Change Schedule • Change windows

Process (...)	Input from TPS to ...	Output from ... to TPS
Change Management cont.	• Prioritize conflicting requirements for Transition resources • Transition lifecycle stages (quality gates – what needs to be achieved to move to next stage) • Acquire/test new CIs/components • Build/test • Service release test • Service operational readiness test • Deployment • ELS • Review and close Transition • Release Policy • RFC for process improvement	• Authorization to advance in the Transition activities
Service Asset and Configuration Management	• Configuration baselines • Integrated set of Transition plans ("holder" of documents and relationships – document CI) • Process activity coordination	• Baseline and evaluation points • Configuration audit; verification
Release and Deployment Management	• Overall ST Policy • Release Policy • Prioritize conflicting requirements for Transition resources • Operational parameters for RDM (policies) • Release design • Current SDP (Service charter, Service model, SAC, etc.) • Activity and resource coordination throughout all Transition activities	• Release Policy • Release plans • Plan, build, test, and deployment of Release package • ELS • Baseline and evaluation points
Service Validation and Testing	• Quality Assurance Plan • Prioritize conflicting requirements for Transition resources • Process activity coordination	• Baselines
Change Evaluation	• Provide necessary resource for Evaluation activities • Process activity coordination	• Resource Request • Evaluation report
Knowledge Management	• Knowledge, information and data around the new/changed Service to be included and managed within the SKMS	• Relevant, timely, required and accurate knowledge, information and data

Process (...)	Input from TPS to ...	Output from ... to TPS
Service Operation		
Event Management		
Incident Management		• Incident handling as related to Transition activities (test/live environments)
Request Fulfillment		•
Problem Management		• RCA as related to Transition activities (test/live environments)
Access Management		
Continual Service Improvement		
7-step Improvement Process	• Tests/reports on monitoring procedures and measurement criteria • Finalizes monitoring procedures for ongoing operations • Identify improvement opportunities	• Recommendations for improvement implantation plans

Function (...)	Input from TPS to ...	Output from ... to TPS
Service Desk		• Service acceptance
Technical Management	• Function activity coordination (pilots, handover, ELS)	• Resources; capabilities
Application Management	• Function activity coordination (pilots, handover, ELS)	• Resources; capabilities
IT Operations Management		• Monitoring/control

Change Management (ChM)

Purpose

Manage the lifecycle of a change, mitigate/reduce risk, and impact to the business within any change activity.

Objectives

- Efficiently/effectively respond to changing business requirements (timely, risk-mitigated/risk accepted, value-driven, and aligned; "Get it right the first time").
- Ensure all changes are properly managed (recorded/documented, assessed, prioritized, scheduled, authorized, planned (including remediation), tested, deployed, and reviewed).
- Ensure all CIs are recorded in the CMS.

Process (...)	Input from ChM to ...	Output from ... to ChM
Service Strategy		
Strategy Management for IT Services	• Approved strategic plans, policies • Actions/plans for cultural, organizational and Service Changes to meet strategic plans	• Mission/vision • Service Strategy • Strategic plans • Policies • Defines changes and the extent of change (ensure change contributes to the achievement of the overall Strategy) • RFC for process improvements
Service Portfolio Management	• Authorizes change proposals and charters • Assesses resources to support change proposals and charters • Mitigates risk to Services as new/changed Service is designed, built, released	• Service charter • Service Portfolio • Service Package descriptions • Service models • Change proposals • Strategic risks • RFCs for improvement (process activities, services, etc.)
Financial Management	• Financial assessment of RFCs • CAB minutes • Resources used in managing the ChM process • Proposed process budget • Approved FM process changes	• Cost of ChM • Inputs on financial impact of a RFC • RFC for process improvement • RFC to improve cost effectiveness • Analysis of change costs (proposed vs actual) • CAB member, if needed • Process budget
Demand Management	• Initiate process activities for new/changed Services which require demand techniques	• Assess impact of changes on how business uses a Service • RFC for process improvements
Business Relationship Management	• Approved changes, charters, proposals • Status of changes	• Change proposal • Service charter • Service requirements

Process (...)	Input from ChM to ...	Output from ... to ChM
Business Relationship Management cont.	• Change Schedule • PSO • Ensured testing • Ensured remediation planning	• Potential risk to customer business from a proposed change • Business impact/urgency information • Schedules of customer activity (change freeze information) • Schedules of training and awareness events • CAB member, if necessary • PIR participation, if necessary • RFC for process improvements
Service Design		
Design Coordination	• Definition of what design efforts required DC efforts • Change in business requirements • RFCs • Change records • Authorized changes • Change Schedule • Change Records • PIR minutes (improvements to DC activities)	• RFC for process improvements • Status information on design activities • Updated Change Records
Service Catalogue Management	• Approved Service Catalogue changes	• RFC updates (impact to Service description/information) • RFC for process improvements
Service Level Management	• CAB agenda/minutes • PSO agreement • RFCs • Change Schedule • Information concerning performance of change both when implemented and subsequently • Receives regular change performance reports • Remediation reports	• PSO negotiation and agreement • RFCs for new/changed Services • Service levels to assist in classifying changes • CAB/ECAB attendance, as appropriate • RFCs for process improvement • Passes user generated RFCs for analysis • Attend CAB • Assesses potential impact of changes on Service quality (disruption of agreed availability/performance, etc.) • Prioritization based on OLAs (IT capabilities) and Service criticality (customer and BRM input) • Impact of RFC on current customers/services (e.g. quality, agreed Service delivery, etc.) • SIPs • RFC for process improvements

Process (...)	Input from ChM to ...	Output from ... to ChM
Availability Management	• Change Schedule • PSO • Changes requiring remediation	• Risk Assessment • PSO contributions • Change Schedule • Planned and preventative maintenance schedule • RFC for process improvements • Assessment of RFCs and their impact on availability • RFCs for analysis • RFCs for process improvements • Change design • Testing plan • Remediation plan input
Capacity Management	• Change Schedule • RFC for CapM assessment • Remediated changes	• RFC impact assessment on current capacity • RFC for capacity improvements • Remediation plan input • RFC for process improvements
IT Service Continuity Management	• RFCs (assess for impact to Continuity Plan) • Change Schedule • Approval to update Continuity Plan	• Assessed RFCs (impact to Continuity Plan) • CAB member, if necessary • ITSCM testing schedule • RFC for process improvements • RFC to update Continuity Plan based on approved changes • RFCs to improve process/continuity measures
Information Security Management	• Authorized changes that have been security assessed • Risk assessment and risk management • Change Schedule	• Member of the CAB/ECAB (potential) • Assessment of RFCs for impact on Security policies • RFCs for process improvements, improved security controls, etc. • Information on unauthorized changes from security breaches
Supplier Management	• Terms/conditions of contacts to assist in scheduling (e.g. procurement times, etc.) • Approved RFCs • Change Schedule	• CAB member (if necessary) • Review of RFCs for impact to contracts • RFC for changed contracts/agreements • Verification of procured components to approved RFC • RFC for process improvements
Service Transition		
Transition Planning and Support	• Change Schedule • Change windows • Authorization to advance in the Transition activities	• Communication Plan • Prioritize conflicting requirements for Transition resources

Process (...)	Input from ChM to ...	Output from ... to ChM
Transition Planning and Support cont.		• Transition lifecycle stages (quality gates – what needs to be achieved to move to next stage) • Acquire/test new CIs/components • Build/test • Service release test • Service operational readiness test • Deployment • ELS • Review and close Transition • Release Policy • RFC for process improvements
Service Asset and Configuration Management	• Scope of CIs under control of ChM process (defines independent change) • Defines depth/breadth of information capture for each CI type/category (Configuration Plan) • Authorization to update CMDB/CI records • CI status, attribute, relationship updates • Change Schedule • Change Records/updates to records • Authorization to remove CI records (CI disposal) • Request for assessment (information validation, etc.) • Approved Service Requests • RFCs • Work orders • PSO • CAB/ECAB meeting minutes and actions • PIR meeting minutes/actions • Contribution to ChM, SACM, RDM plan	• Information to assess impact of RFC • Status reports • CI verification and audit information • RFC for process improvements • Change status • Baseline information • CI owners (i.e. information to determine who to consult for RFC impact, etc.) • Assistance in determining who needs to be consulted within any specific RFC • Details of CAB/ECAB members • Matching RFCs to impacted CIs to ensure minimize/eliminate conflict • Register and update all RFCs and change records • Configuration audit discrepancies • CAB/ECAB details
Release and Deployment Management	• Authorized change • Change Schedule • PSO information • CAB meeting minutes • Required/ensured testing • Required/ensured remediation plan • Authorization for Release Build • Authorization for Deployment	• Release Policy • Release Plan • Deployment Plan • Testing Plan • Release test results • Tested release package for authorization to deploy • Deploys approved change (Release)

Process (...)	Input from ChM to ...	Output from ... to ChM
Release and Deployment Management cont.	• Authorization for release to DML • Operational review procedures • PIR procedures	• Operational review information • Review of Deployment (input to PIR) • Recommendation for Remediation • Remediation Plan input • Remediation results • Updates on RDM activities • Release plans to impact Change Schedule • Release acceptance documents • RFC for process improvement
Service Validation and Testing	• Authorized RFCs for testing activities	• Testing Plan • Test results • RFC for process improvements
Change Evaluation	• Request for Evaluation • RFCs • Change Records • Definition of change types that will require formal Evaluation • Change Schedule (includes Evaluation activities)	• Evaluation Plan (timing of activities to coincide with change/release activities) • Interim Evaluation reports • Final Evaluation Report • RFC for process improvements
Knowledge Management	• Accurate capture, store, use and manage process information and data	• Relevant, timely, required and accurate knowledge, information and data • RFC for process improvements
Service Operation		
Event Management		• RFC for assessment (based on monitoring thresholds and defined events) • RFC for process improvements • RFC for event-related change • Events that trigger change actions
Incident Management	• Change Schedule • Details of implemented changes (Change Records) • Authorized emergency changes • PSO • Approved emergency changes details	• Change-related incidents • RFC for incident resolution • RFC for improved process
Request Fulfillment	• Approved standard changes	• RFCs for standard change • RFC for process improvements
Problem Management	• Change Schedule • PSO • CAB agenda • CAB minutes • Status on changes that resolve problems • History of changes that have been remediated • Approved emergency changes	• Member of the CAB • Problems associated to change • PIR criteria • PIR participation • RFC for process improvements • Latest information concerning RFC priority

Process (…)	Input from ChM to …	Output from … to ChM
Problem Management cont.	• PIR procedures • Details of implemented changes (for RCA activities) • Approved emergency changes	• RFC for problem resolution (as well as permanently correct KEs)
Access Management	• Approved access control actions	• RFC for access control modification • RFC for process improvements
Continual Service Improvement		
7-step Improvement Process	• Results of RFC, proposal, charter assessment (approved/rejected) • Change Schedule • Identify improvement opportunities	• Improvement RFCs, charters, and proposals • Participate in CAB/PIR meetings, if necessary • Recommendations for improvement implantation plans

Function (…)	Input from ChM to …	Output from … to ChM
Service Desk	• Change Schedule • PSO information	• Change-related incidents • RFCs on behalf of caller • RFCs to improve process at Service Desk
Technical Management	• Approval of maintenance/operational changes (standard) • Change Schedule	• Submission of RFC for operational activities • CAB member, if necessary • Communication of Service operation concerns for RFCs • Evaluation of RFCs, if needed • Implementation of authorized change • Backing out changes/application of Remediation Plan, if necessary • Move physical assets within enterprise as needed • Define/maintain Change models
Application Management	• Approval of maintenance/operational changes (standard) • Change Schedule	• Submission of RFC for operational activities • CAB member, if necessary • Communication of Service operation concerns for RFCs • Evaluation of RFCs, if needed • Implementation of authorized change • Backing out changes/application of remediation plan, if necessary • Move physical assets within enterprise as needed

Function (...)	Input from ChM to ...	Output from ... to ChM
Application Management cont.		• Define/maintain change models
IT Operations Management	• Change Schedule	• RFCs • CAB member, if necessary • Communication of Service operation concerns for RFCs • Move physical assets within enterprise as needed • Backing out changes/application of remediation plan, if necessary

Service Asset and Configuration Management (SACM)

Purpose

Ensure that reliable, accurate (configurations, relationships), and controlled information on assets required to deliver Services is available as needed (timely, accessible, etc.).

Objectives

- Ensure IT-controlled assets are identified, controlled, maintained over the asset's lifecycle.
- Manage (e.g. identify, control, record, report, audit, verify, etc.) CIs (services, hardware, software, data, environment, documents, people) over their lifecycle via the capture and maintenance of relationships, versions, baselines, attributes, etc.
- Capture, control, and maintain information (current, planned, historical) on CIs within a CMS.
- Ensure a proper interface and change control over CIs and their associated configuration.
- Provide accurate and timely information to Service Management processes to support process decisions.

Process (...)	Input from SACM to ...	Output from ... to SACM
Service Strategy		
Strategy Management for IT Services	• Use/deployment of corporate assets/CIs	• Mission/vision • Service Strategy • Policies • Process artifacts recorded as CIs
Service Portfolio Management	• CMS supports the Service Portfolio and all its components • Provides data/information for Service models • Relationships between CIs, Service Assets and Service delivery	• "Documents" managed via the CMDB/CMS (recorded as CIs)
Financial Management	• CMS/CMDB • Details for cost model development • CI relationships for IT Accounting • Charging algorithms • CI details (e.g. purchase price, depreciation, replacement, etc.) • CI lifecycle information for replacement budgeting and future planning	• CI purchase price, current value, depreciation to date, replacement price, etc. • Cost model details • Storing of budgeting and IT accounting information • Charging algorithms • Service Catalogue prices • CI owners • Purchase and upgrade replacement date

Process (...)	Input from SACM to ...	Output from ... to SACM
Financial Management cont.	• Resources used to manage the SACM process • Proposed process budget • Updated information for the asset register • Provides repository to capture cost, depreciation methods, owners, users, maintenance, repair costs, etc.	• Purchase Orders • Acquisitions • Asset Register • SACM process budget/cost • Define financial attribute fields (with corporate finance)
Demand Management	• Identify relationship between Service demand and demand on systems/devices	• PBAs/UPs (document CI)
Business Relationship Management	• Critical documents (e.g. history, data, etc.) held within the CMDB	• Stakeholders • Service Customers
Service Design		
Design Coordination	• CMS, CMDB	• SDP
Service Catalogue Management	• CMDB identifies all items within a Service, which might be helpful in developing a Service Catalogue	• Service Catalogue for Service CI definition (include in CMS; link CIs)
Service Level Management	• Relationships between Services, Service Assets, CIs and customers • Holds SLM documents as CIs • CMDB useful when developing improvement plans • Shows components within a Service which may help justify Service costs • CMDB useful in developing SIP	• Service information • SLRs, SLAs, OLAs, SIPs. SLAM documents to be included as CIs • Relationships between SLAs/OLAs/UCs, etc. • Information on access to CI records
Availability Management	• Relationship information • Technical information (topology, CI relationships) • Relationship information for use in availability/design activities • Basis for CFIA, FTA, identification of SPOFs and other weaknesses • Details of CIs that need to be risk managed as part of the Availability Plan • License usage/availability • AMIS links	• AMIS • Relationships between CIs (resilience) • Availability Plan (as a CI and informational purposes) • BIA results (with ITSCM) • Risk assessment results (with ITSCM, ISM) • Risk reduction measures (with ITSCM, ISM) • Availability activity (CFIA, FTA, SFA, Incident lifecycle analysis, etc.) results
Capacity Management	• CMS/CMDB • Technical topology/architectures • Identification of potential bottlenecks or other points of weakness	• CMIS • Capacity Plan as a document CI • Performance information may be a CI attribute

Process (...)	Input from SACM to ...	Output from ... to SACM
Capacity Management cont.	• Knowledge of the relationships between Service elements could be important if there are capacity problems • CMIS links	
IT Service Continuity Management	• CMS/CMDB • Continuity baseline • Critical components/services to be included in Continuity Plan • Configuration details of alternate/failover services/environments • Full version control details of the ITSCM Plan • Configuration details of alternative Services to be used in a disaster • Up-to-date information about the content of the infrastructure	• ITSCM configuration baseline • Continuity Plan (document CI)
Information Security Management	• CMS/CMDB • Relationships between Service components from a ISM view	• SMIS links • Information on access to CI records • Security controls • Security Policy • Supporting ISM-based policies (access, password, email, internet, anti-virus, etc.) • Access control information (AM) • Security checks/tests to ensure proper access to CMDB/CMS is attained/followed • Security checks on access to the DML
Supplier Management	• CMS/CMDB	• SCMIS • Warranty information • POC for supplier • Contract details • Supplier details • Information on new CIs • Other CI attributes

Process (...)	Input from SACM to ...	Output from ... to SACM
Service Transition		
Transition Planning and Support	• Baseline and evaluation points • Configuration audit; verification	• Configuration baselines • Integrated set of Transition plans ("holder" of documents and relationships – document CI) • Process activity coordination
Change Management	• Information to assess impact of RFC • Status reports • CI verification and audit information • RFC for process improvements • Change status • Baseline information • CI owners (i.e. information to determine who to consult for RFC impact, etc) • Assistance in determining who needs to be consulted within any specific RFC • Details of CAB/ECAB members • Matching RFCs to impacted CIs to ensure minimize/eliminate conflict • Register and update all RFCs and Change Records • Configuration audit discrepancies • CAB/ECAB details	• Scope of CIs under control of ChM process (defines independent change) • Defines depth/breadth of information capture for each CI type/category (Configuration Plan) • Authorization to update CMDB/CI records • CI status, attribute, relationship updates • Change Schedule • Change records/updates to records • Authorization to remove CI records (CI disposal) • Request for assessment (information validation, etc.) • Approved Service Requests • RFCs • Work Orders • PSO • CAB/ECAB meeting minutes and actions • PIR meeting minutes/actions • Contribution to ChM, SACM, RDM plan
Release and Deployment Management	• Release records • Configuration of current release • Authorization of access to DML • License information • CI owners/maintainers/suppliers • CI audits (pre-/post-release) • CI information for delta Releases • Basic information on each CI (attributes – versions, location, etc.) • Assists in roll-out activities (where, to whom, when, etc.) • Assists in finding illegal/unauthorized CIs	• Updated CI information • Release and Deployment plans • Information on DML CIs • Decommissioned/retired CIs • DML audit results (pre-/post-release) • Contribution to ChM, SACM, RDM Plans • Baseline capture prior to release • Updated information on Release Package stored in DML

Process (...)	Input from SACM to ...	Output from ... to SACM
Release and Deployment Management cont.	• Defines secure stores for warehousing IT assets (definitive spares; DML) • Ensures only authorized media is stored in DML • Defines the configuration of the DML • Baselines • CI owners • May assist in distribution of release (physically or logically)	
Service Validation and Testing	• Access to DML for stored testing data, scripts, configurations, etc.	• Configuration baseline from test environment • Repository for test data, scripts, test configurations, etc. (DML) • Repository for results
Change Evaluation	• Data, information for Evaluation activities	• Repository for process artifacts (document CIs)
Knowledge Management	• CMS/CMDB links • Accurate capture, store, use and manage process information and data	• SKMS links • Relevant, timely, required and accurate knowledge, information and data (SKMS)
Service Operation		
Event Management	• Event records (historical) • New CIs which will be monitored • CI baselines in CMS for comparison of current event	• Event records • CIs related to an event • CI information to update lifecycle status
Incident Management	• CI identification • CI relationships • User/caller information • CI owners, maintainers, suppliers • CI status/history • CI warranty information • CI location • CI details for classification, matching, prioritization • CI escalation information • Problem/KE information • Workarounds • Scripts • Provides/maintains diagnostic information • Provides historical view of Incidents • CI status/history • CI warranty information • CI location	• Incident records/updates • CMDB errors • CI attribute/relationships updates • Resolution/closure details • CI status updates

Process (...)	Input from SACM to ...	Output from ... to SACM
Request Fulfillment	• Service Request records (historical) • Process documentation (request models, workflows, etc.)	• Service Requests • CI updates
Problem Management	• CI identification • CI relationships • CI owners, maintainers, suppliers • User/customer information • CI details for classification, matching, prioritization • CI escalation information • Problem/KE records • Information for trend analysis • CI status/history • Incident history (for diagnosis purposes) • Provides/maintains diagnostic information • Provides historical view of Problems • Relationships between CIs for root cause analysis	• KEs • KEDB links • Workaround information • CI status updates • Problem records and updates
Access Management	• Access control information (ISM/AM)	• Access controls for CIs • Profile/user attribute definitions
Continual Service Improvement		
7-step Improvement Process	• Benchmark data • Baseline data • Identify improvement opportunities	• Recommendations for improvement implantation plans

Function (...)	Input from SACM to ...	Output from ... to SACM
Service Desk	• Information to properly assess incident (classification, prioritization, scope, impact, etc.)	• Updated incident record • Updated CI record, where authorized
Technical Management	• CI Owner confirmation • Request for assistance in maintaining CMS	• Discrepancies between infrastructure and CMDB • Correcting CI records, with authorization • Labeling/tagging physical assets/CIs • Perform audits • System/operational process/procedures

Function (...)	Input from SACM to ...	Output from ... to SACM
Technical Management cont.		• Updating CMS, with authorization (relationships, add new CIs, confirm status, etc.) • Maintenance schedules • Technical manuals • Management/administration manuals
Application Management	• CI owner confirmation • Request for assistance in maintaining CMS	• Discrepancies between infrastructure and CMDB • Correcting CI records, with authorization • Labeling/tagging physical assets/CIs • Perform audits • Updating CMS, with authorization (relationships, add new CIs, confirm status, etc.) • Maintenance schedules • Manuals • Management/administration manuals • Requirements documents • Use cases • Design documents
IT Operations Management	• Request for assistance in maintaining CMS	• Discrepancies between infrastructure and CMDB • Correcting CI records, with authorization • Labeling/tagging physical assets/CIs • Perform audits • Updating CMS, with authorization (relationships, add new CIs, confirm status, etc.) • Process/procedure documentation • Operation logs • Shift schedules/reports • Operation Schedule

Release and Deployment Management (RDM)

Purpose

To protect Service integrity as approved new/changed functionality is delivered via appropriate and managed (plan, schedule, control) build, test, and deployment of Releases.

Objectives

- Create/agree Release and Deployment plans with customers/stakeholders.
- Create/test Release packages (related and compatible CIs).
- Maintain Release package integrity throughout Transition activities (store in DML; record in CMS).
- Only deploy Release packages from DML following agreed plan/schedule.
- Ensure all Release packages can be tracked, installed, tested, and uninstalled/backed out.
- Ensure holistic approach is followed during a release (e.g. organizational change, training, knowledge transfer, health/safety, etc) for both customers/users as well as operational personnel.
- Ensure agreed utility/warranty can be met via the new/changed Service (SVT, ChE).
- Acknowledge/manage deviations, risks, and issues with appropriate corrective actions.

Process (...)	Input from RDM to ...	Output from ... to RDM
Service Strategy		
Strategy Management for IT Services	• Actions and plans for cultural, organizational and Service Changes to meet strategic plans • Service Transition Report • Release policies	• Mission/vision • Service Strategy • Policies • Application Portfolio • Guidance for Release Policy development based on overall strategic view
Service Portfolio Management	• New Service (information) to Service Catalogue (SCatM)	• Service Portfolio (Service Catalogue, Service Pipeline, Retired Services)
Financial Management	• Release Plans (support accounting for new, changed or retired Service Deployment) • Resources used in managing the RDM process • Proposed process budget	• Cost of RDM • Deployment option costs • Analysis of Service asset costs • Procurement of Service assets as needed
Demand Management	• Release plans	• Impact of release plan on current demand constraints
Business Relationship Management	• New/changed Service Deployment • Service notification • Release Policy • Release Plan	• Defined business outcomes • Service requirements • Schedule of customer activity • Schedule of training and awareness events

Process (...)	Input from RDM to ...	Output from ... to RDM
Business Relationship Management cont.		• Input when establishing Release Policies to ensure policies reflect business need • Input during planning to ensure business operations are not negatively impacted during a release
Service Design		
Design Coordination	• Plan/design of Release and Deployment of new/changed Service for inclusion to the SDP	• Ensure planning and design of Release units and Deployment actions are integrated into overall design (SDP)
Service Catalogue Management	• Information on deployed changes to a Service in the Service Catalogue (update information for that Service)	• Service Catalogue (to understand the overall nature of all Services)
Service Level Management	• Release Policies • Release Plans • Information to update SLAs/OLAs • Information to update Service reports • Request for users in UAT testing	• SLRs (input when establishing Release Policies) • Confirmation that defined users are available for implementation and/or distribution of a release, as planned and agreed
Availability Management	• Release Schedule • Release Plans	• Risk assessment • Input to Release Schedule • Service Designs • Build models/plans • Test plans • Identification of any availability issue during release planning • Immediate identification of any availability issue during a release
Capacity Management	• Release Plans • Information to update Capacity Plan	• Service Designs • Build models/plans • Identification of any capacity issue during release planning • Immediate identification of any capacity issue during a release
IT Service Continuity Management	• Plans for deploying Services into the failover environment (post invocation of the Continuity Plan) • Tested Continuity Plans	• Identification of Continuity issues (Release Plan) • Continuity Plan • Immediate identification of any Continuity issue during a release
Information Security Management	• Release Policy • Release Plans (confirmation of security measures to protect release of CIs)	• Define the secure handling of CIs as per the Security Policy within the Release Policy

Process (...)	Input from RDM to ...	Output from ... to RDM
Information Security Management cont.		• Confirmation that Release package meets necessary security standards as per Security Policy
Supplier Management	• Requirements for CI delivery • Information to update UCs	• Terms/conditions for suppliers allowing good Release planning • Participation in Deployment, as contracted
Service Transition		
Transition Planning and Support	• Release Policy • Release Plans • Plan, build, test, and deployment of Release package • ELS • Baseline and evaluation points	• Overall ST Policy • Release Policy • Prioritize conflicting requirements for Transition resources • Operational parameters for RDM (policies) • Release design • Current SDP (Service charter, Service model, SAC, etc.) • Activity and resource coordination throughout all Transition activities
Change Management	• Release Policy • Release Plan • Deployment Plan • Testing Plan • Release test results • Tested Release package for authorization to deploy • Deploys approved change (Release) • Operational review information • Review of Deployment (input to PIR) • Recommendation for remediation • Remediation Plan input • Remediation results • Updates on RDM activities • Release Plans to impact Change Schedule • Release acceptance documents • RFC for process improvement	• Authorized change • Change Schedule • PSO information • CAB meeting minutes • Required/ensured testing • Required/ensured Remediation Plan • Authorization for Release build • Authorization for Deployment • Authorization for Release to DML • Operational review procedures • PIR procedures
Service Asset and Configuration Management	• Updated CI information • Release and Deployment Plans • Information on DML CIs • Decommissioned/retired CIs • DML audit results (pre-/post-Release) • Contribution to ChM, SACM, RDM Plans	• Release records • Configuration of current Release • Authorization of access to DML • License information • CI owners/maintainers/suppliers • CI audits (pre-/post-Release)

Process (...)	Input from RDM to ...	Output from ... to RDM
Service Asset and Configuration Management cont.	• Baseline capture prior to Release • Updated information on Release package stored in DML	• CI information for delta Releases • Basic information on each CI (attributes – versions, location, etc) • Assists in roll-out activities (where, to whom, when, etc) • Assists in finding illegal/unauthorized CIs • Defines secure stores for warehousing IT assets (definitive spares; DML) • Ensures only authorized media is stored in DML • Defines the configuration of the DML • Baselines • CI owners • May assist in distribution of release (physically or logically)
Service Validation and Testing	• Release Plan • Test Plan • Release package for defined testing	• Validation of Release package • Validation of Service models • Release package test results especially UAT • Control over live test environment
Change Evaluation	• Release Policy • Release Plans	• Provides necessary Evaluation results prior to ChM authorization to progress through RDM activities (significant changes only)
Knowledge Management	• Defines knowledge capture for new/changed Services • Defines necessary knowledge transfer in relation to new/changed Services	• Relevant, timely, required and accurate knowledge, information and data
Service Operation		
Event Management		• Information indicating completion of standard deployments, if configured
Incident Management	• Release Plan (roll-out Strategy) • Deployment Plan • Diagnostic scripts • Ensure Service acceptance • ELS parameters • Ensure proper training for correct support capabilities • When a change has been fully deployed • Issues associated with testing failures which are tracked as incidents	• Details of unexpected post-release events • Service Acceptance document (Service Desk)

Process (...)	Input from RDM to ...	Output from ... to RDM
Request Fulfillment	• Automated Deployment mechanisms for specified requests	• Workflow for standard changes to be validated by RDM
Problem Management	• Evidence to close problem records • Pre-release KEs • PIR criteria • Development KEs to live/operation KEDB	• Details of all identified post-Release problems
Access Management		
Continual Service Improvement		
7-step Improvement Process	• Deployment of approved improvement • Identify improvement opportunities	• Recommendations for improvement implantation plans

Function (...)	Input from RDM to ...	Output from ... to RDM
Service Desk	• Release Policy • Release Plans • Service notification (Service Desk) • Ensure proper training for correct support capabilities • Early life support as per Release Policy	• Service Acceptance sign-off indicating ready to support new/changed Service • Release-related incidents
Technical Management	• Release Policies • Release Plans	• Technical expertise for planning a Release • Communicate Service operation issues • Distribution/installation/implementation of authorized Releases to live environment • Perform back-out/remediation tasks, as needed • Physically handling/moving CIs throughout enterprise as needed
Application Management	• Release Policies • Release Plans • Final authority on build management and integration testing • Software released from DML • DML may point to a definitive hardware store	• Input to Release Policy and Plan • Master copies of software (and related artifacts) to DML • Provide all appropriate operational management information (e.g. KEs, Release notes, etc.) prior to live operation • Distribution/installation/implementation of authorized Releases to live environment • Perform back-out/remediation tasks, as needed

Function (...)	Input from RDM to ...	Output from ... to RDM
IT Operations Management	• Release Policies • Release Plans	• Facilities will ensure access to various locations for Deployment • Accept delivery of CIs and securely store CIs until needed within the Release Plan • Physically handling/moving CIs throughout enterprise as needed

Service Validation and Testing (SVT)

Purpose

Ensure the new/change Service Design meets specification and needs of the business.

Objectives

- Evidence that a Release package will deliver expected outcomes.
- Quality assurance of the Release package, Service CIs, Service capability.
- Ensure stated utility and warranty will be met.
- Measure against Service requirements throughout Transition design/process and remedy errors "earlier rather than later."
- Identify, manage, and control risk throughout Transition activities.

Process (...)	Input from SVT to ...	Output from ... to SVT
Service Strategy		
Strategy Management for IT Services	• Actions and plans for cultural, organizational and Service Changes to meet strategic plans	• Mission/vision • Service Strategy • Policies • Parameters for testing to ensure achievement of strategic objectives • Appropriate recognition, funding, resources, and communication around testing
Service Portfolio Management	• Confirmation of Service functionality based on testing activities • Confirmation of anticipated Service return	• Strategic risks
Financial Management	• Test activities/resources for invoicing/billing/cost of Service • Proposed process budget	• Cost of SVT
Demand Management	• Validate PBAs via testing • Validate methods of preventing over-utilization of resources • Request for input to test scenarios for managing future demand	• Proposed/known Service resource limits • Techniques used to be included in testing
Business Relationship Management	• Results of UAT	• SAC • Customer requirements • Confirmation of test requirements

Process (...)	Input from SVT to ...	Output from ... to SVT
Service Design		
Design Coordination	• Plan/design of Service test requirements for inclusion to the SDP • Test capabilities/resources	• Ensure planning and design of tests are integrated into overall design (SDP) • SDP (Service charter, Service provide interface definitions, operation models, capacity/resource model/plans, financial models (TCO, TCU, etc.), SM model, test conditions (expected results), design/interface specifications, Release/Deployment plans, acceptance criteria
Service Catalogue Management		
Service Level Management		• Service targets (as test targets)
Availability Management	• Test results • Validation/verification of SAC	• Risk assessment • Tests (resilience, failover, etc)
Capacity Management	• Confirmation of capacity requirement fulfillment during validation/testing activities	• Capacity-related input to testing requirements and planning (e.g. software licensing, service staffing requirements, etc.)
IT Service Continuity Management	• Test results	• Testing requirements/parameters • ITSCM testing schedule • TISCM test scenarios
Information Security Management	• Reports on security-related testing	• Security Policy around test data • Security Policy as applied to the test environment
Supplier Management	• Test results of third party assets	
Service Transition		
Transition Planning and Support	• Baselines	• Quality Assurance Plan • Prioritize conflicting requirements for Transition resources • Process activity coordination
Change Management	• Test Plan • Test results • RFC for process improvements	• Authorized RFCs for testing activities

Process (...)	Input from SVT to ...	Output from ... to SVT
Service Asset and Configuration Management	• Configuration baseline from test environment • Repository for test data, scripts, test configurations, etc. (DML) • Repository for results	• Access to DML for stored testing data, scripts, configurations, etc.
Release and Deployment Management	• Validation of Release package • Validation of Service models • Release package test results especially UAT • Control over live test environment	• Release Plan • Test Plan • Release package for defined testing
Change Evaluation	• Test results, analysis, report	•
Knowledge Management	• Accurately capture, store, use and manage process information and data	• Relevant, timely, required and accurate knowledge, information and data
Service Operation		
Event Management		
Incident Management	• Known issues with a change to be deployed with options for resolving incidents	• Test incidents (if IM is active in the development/test environment)
Request Fulfillment	• Results of tests around workflow	
Problem Management	• Test problems (request for formal investigation)	• RCA of test errors because of procedure/protocol or unexpected results
Access Management	• Test results of access control measures	• Testing of Service access requirements, etc.
Continual Service Improvement		
7-step Improvement Process	• Identify improvement opportunities • Service improvement opportunities (from failed tests)	• Process improvement opportunities • Recommendations for improvement implantation plans

Function (...)	Input from SVT to ...	Output from ... to SVT
Service Desk		
Technical Management	• Operational tests	• Actual performance data for analysis
Application Management	• Operational tests	• Actual performance data for analysis
IT Operations Management		

111

Change Evaluation (ChE)

Purpose

Via consistent and standardized methods, assess the impact of a new/changed Service on existing/proposed Services and infrastructure with the goal of achieving business outcome (value).

Objectives

- Provide efficient and effective feedback to ChM-evaluated new/changed Services; especially those that could potentially introduce unacceptable levels of risk.
- Evaluate the intended and unintended effects of a new/changed Service, within practical reason.
- Provide clear and definitive reports enabling quick/accurate decision-making (authorization) by ChM.

Process (...)	Input from ChE to ...	Output from ... to ChE
Service Strategy		
Strategy Management for IT Services	• Any agreed variation from original intent feed back into Strategy for adjustments and validation	• Mission/vision • Service Strategy • Policies • Information to prioritize and evaluate Services ensuring they are built to original intent
Service Portfolio Management	• Interim/final ChE reports (ChM)	• Change proposal • Requirements/risks which are used to assess the new/changed Service
Financial Management	• Resources used in managing the ChE process • Proposed process budget	• Cost of ChE • Cost:Risk analysis
Demand Management	• Recommendations on demand based on change trends	
Business Relationship Management	• Resource for answer customer/user questions around Evaluation activities of new/changed Service • Interim/final Evaluation reports (to report to customer)	• Customer risk information • Customer requirements • Request by stakeholder for evaluation • Impact assessment of issues identified from Evaluation • Customers/users to participate in Evaluation activities, if needed

Process (...)	Input from ChE to ...	Output from ... to ChE
Service Design		
Design Coordination	• Evaluation of Service Design (how well it meets stated requirements)	• SDP (Service charter, SAC, etc.) • Ensure SDP contains accurate and up-to-date information to assist ChE activities
Service Catalogue Management		• Services in the Service Catalogue and impact criteria for the Services
Service Level Management	• Resource for answering customer/user questions around Evaluation activities of new/changed Service	• Impact assessment of issues identified from Evaluation • Customers/users to participate in Evaluation activities, if needed
Availability Management		• The availability thresholds for Evaluation reports
Capacity Management		• The capacity thresholds for Evaluation reports
IT Service Continuity Management	• Assessment of Continuity Plans as per Service Designs	• Continuity Plans • Continuity test plans/results
Information Security Management		
Supplier Management		
Service Transition		
Transition Planning and Support	• Resource Request • Evaluation Report	• Provide necessary resource for Evaluation activities • Process activity coordination
Change Management	• Evaluation Plan (timing of activities to coincide with Change/Release activities) • Interim Evaluation reports • Final Evaluation Report • RFC for process improvements	• Request for Evaluation • RFCs • Change Records • Definition of change types that will require formal evaluation • Change Schedule (includes Evaluation activities)
Service Asset and Configuration Management	• Repository for process artifacts (document CIs)	• Data, information for Evaluation activities
Release and Deployment Management	• Provides necessary evaluation results prior to ChM authorization to progress through RDM activities (significant changes only)	• Release Policy • Release Plan

Process (...)	Input from ChE to ...	Output from ... to ChE
Service Validation and Testing		• Test results, analysis, report
Knowledge Management	• Accurate capture, store, use and manage process information and data	• Relevant, timely, required and accurate knowledge, information and data
Service Operation		
Event Management		• Data for Evaluation reports
Incident Management		• Data for Evaluation reports (failures of new/changed Service)
Request Fulfillment		
Problem Management		• Data for Evaluation reports (failures of new/changed Service)
Access Management		
Continual Service Improvement		
7-step Improvement Process	• Identify improvement opportunities	• Recommendations for improvement implantation plans

Function (...)	Input from ChE to ...	Output from ... to ChE
Service Desk		
Technical Management	• Perform Evaluation activities (data collection)	• Evaluation activities and data analysis
Application Management	• Perform Evaluation activities (data collection)	• Evaluation activities and data analysis
IT Operations Management		

Knowledge Management (KM)

Purpose

Provide the right information, at the right time, to the right people to support decision-making and reduce the need to re-discover information (accurate and timely repository structure).

Objectives

- Improve management decision-making quality (right information, right time, right people).
- Maintain a SKMS where access is controlled (managed and secure).
- Gather, analyze, store, share, use, and maintain appropriate/required knowledge, information, data.

Process (...)	Input from KM to ...	Output from ... to KM
Service Strategy		
Strategy Management for IT Services	• Structures information for use in strategic decisions (understand environment, history, dynamics, etc) • Relevant, timely, required, and accurate knowledge, information, and data (SKMS)	• Mission/vision • Service Strategy • Policies • Accurately capture, store, use, and manage process information and data
Service Portfolio Management	• Relevant, timely, required, and accurate knowledge, information, and data (SKMS)	• Service Portfolio (Service Pipeline, Service Catalogue, Retired Services) • Market space research • Risk research • Various portfolios • Accurately capture, store, use, and manage process information and data • Update of Service Portfolio
Financial Management	• Resources used in managing the KM process • Proposed process budget • Relevant, timely, required, and accurate knowledge, information, and data (SKMS)	• Cost of KM • Appropriate financial data, information, knowledge • Accurately capture, store, use, and manage process information and data
Demand Management	• Relevant, timely, required, and accurate knowledge, information, and data (SKMS)	• Accurately capture, store, use, and manage process information and data
Business Relationship Management	• Relevant, timely, required, and accurate knowledge, information, and data (SKMS)	• Knowledge capture around customer business/requirements • Accurately capture, store, use, and manage process information and data • Store minutes of customer meetings

Process (...)	Input from KM to ...	Output from ... to KM
Service Design		
Design Coordination	• Relevant, timely, required, and accurate knowledge, information, and data (SKMS)	• Accurately capture, store, use, and manage process information and data • Update of SDP • Knowledge, information and data around the new/changed Service to be included and managed within the SKMS
Service Catalogue Management	• Relevant, timely, required, and accurate knowledge, information, and data (SKMS) • Standards for managing the information regarding the Services in the Service Catalogue	• Accurately capture, store, use, and manage process information and data • Updated Service Catalogue
Service Level Management	• Relevant, timely, required, and accurate knowledge, information, and data (SKMS) • Expectations of maintaining any Service-related knowledge	• Accurately capture, store, use, and manage process information and data • Store minutes of customer meeting • Service review meeting minutes • Customer report
Availability Management	• Relevant, timely, required, and accurate knowledge, information, and data	• Accurately capture, store, use, and manage process information and data • New/changed Availability Plan
Capacity Management	• Relevant, timely, required, and accurate knowledge, information, and data (SKMS)	• Accurately capture, store, use, and manage process information and data • New/changed Capacity Plan
IT Service Continuity Management	• Past test results • Test information • Test scenarios • Information that may impact tests or invocation of Continuity Plan • Relevant, timely, required, and accurate knowledge, information, and data (SKMS)	• Post-testing/invocation information and lessons learned • Accurately capture, store, use, and manage process information and data • New/changed Continuity Plan
Information Security Management	• Relevant, timely, required, and accurate knowledge, information, and data (SKMS)	• Security check on access to SKMS/CMS/CMDB • Accurately capture, store, use, and manage process information and data • New/changed Security controls/policies

Process (...)	Input from KM to ...	Output from ... to KM
Supplier Management	• SCMIS (relationship information; contact details, etc.) • Relevant, timely, required, and accurate knowledge, information, and data (SKMS)	• SCMIS • Supplier knowledgebase • Accurately capture, store, use, and manage process information and data • Delivery of user information
Service Transition		
Transition Planning and Support	• Relevant, timely, required, and accurate knowledge, information, and data (SKMS)	• Knowledge, information, and data around the new/changed Service to be included and managed within the SKMS
Change Management	• Relevant, timely, required, and accurate knowledge, information, and data (SKMS) • RFC for process improvements	• Accurately capture, store, use, and manage process information and data
Service Asset and Configuration Management	• SKMS links • Relevant, timely, required, and accurate knowledge, information, and data (SKMS)	• CMS/CMDB links • Accurately capture, store, use, and manage process information and data
Release and Deployment Management	• Relevant, timely, required, and accurate knowledge, information, and data (SKMS)	• Defines knowledge capture for new/changed Services • Defines necessary knowledge transfer in relation to new/changed Services
Service Validation and Testing	• Relevant, timely, required, and accurate knowledge, information, and data (SKMS)	• Accurately capture, store, use, and manage process information and data
Change Evaluation	• Relevant, timely, required, and accurate knowledge, information, and data (SKMS)	• Accurately capture, store, use, and manage process information and data
Service Operation		
Event Management	• Relevant, timely, required, and accurate knowledge, information, and data (SKMS)	• Additions to the DIKW structure (event-related) of the SKMS
Incident Management	• Knowledge regarding Services for understanding and troubleshooting incidents • Ensures availability/accuracy of information for knowledge transfer in new or revised support procedures • Relevant, timely, required, and accurate knowledge, information, and data (SKMS)	• Accurately capture, store, use, and manage process information and data • Capture of SM data • Fully described actions by support analysts
Request Fulfillment	• Fulfill information requests • Relevant, timely, required, and accurate knowledge, information, and data (SKMS)	• Accurately capture, store, use, and manage process information and data

Process (...)	Input from KM to ...	Output from ... to KM
Problem Management	• Relevant, timely, required, and accurate knowledge, information, and data (SKMS)	• Accurately capture, store, use, and manage process information and data • Scripts to assist data capture by IM staff for resolution or further analysis • KEDB links (via CMDB/CMS)
Access Management	• Relevant, timely, required, and accurate knowledge, information, and data (SKMS)	• Provide access rights to the SKMS based on ISM/AM policies • General information for organization around access (grant, revoke, reduce, change)
Continual Service Improvement		
7-step Improvement Process	• Relevant, timely, required, and accurate knowledge, information, and data (SKMS) • Process improvement opportunities	• Updated CSI Register • Accurate capture, store, and use of management process information and data • Recommendations for improvement implantation plans

Function (...)	Input from KM to ...	Output from ... to KM
Service Desk	• Relevant, timely, required, and accurate knowledge, information, and data	• Capture of SM data
Technical Management	• Utilize previously captured and stored data to make corrections within a Transition and NOT repeat prior errors • Relevant, timely, required, and accurate knowledge, information, and data	• Data capture throughout Transition activities for analysis, trending, historical purposes • Operational knowledge capture
Application Management	• Utilize previously captured and stored data to make corrections within a Transition and NOT repeat prior errors • Relevant, timely, required, and accurate knowledge, information, and data	• Data capture throughout Transition activities for analysis, trending, historical purposes
IT Operations Management	• Relevant, timely, required, and accurate knowledge, information, and data	• Accurately capture, store, use, and manage activity information and data • Process/procedure documents for managing IT Operations Control events and facility events

Service Operation (SO)

Purpose

Perform the necessary process-driven activities to deliver, support, and manage Services at the agreed level including continuing management of the supporting technologies.

Objectives

- Maintain (improve) business satisfaction and confidence in IT Services.
- Minimize impact of outages that cannot be proactively prevented.
- Ensure Services are accessible only to those authorized to utilize them.

Lifecycle Phase (…)	Input from SO to …	Output from … to SO
Service Strategy	<ul><li>Operating risks</li><li>Operating cost information for TCO calculations</li><li>Actual performance data</li></ul>	<ul><li>Vision and mission</li><li>Service Portfolio</li><li>Policies</li><li>Strategies and strategic plans</li><li>Priorities</li><li>Financial information and budgets</li><li>Demand forecasts and strategies</li><li>Strategic risks</li></ul>
Service Design	<ul><li>Operational requirements</li><li>Actual performance data</li><li>RFCs to resolve operational issues</li><li>Historical incident and problem records</li></ul>	<ul><li>Service Catalogue</li><li>SDPs, including:<ul><li>Details of utility and warranty</li><li>Operations plans and procedures</li><li>Recovery procedures</li></ul></li><li>Knowledge and information in the SKMS</li><li>Vital business functions</li><li>HW/SW maintenance requirements</li><li>Designs for SO processes and procedures</li><li>SLAs, OLAs, UCs</li><li>Security policies</li></ul>
Service Transition	<ul><li>RFCs to resolve operational issues</li><li>Feedback on quality of Transition activities</li><li>Input to operational testing</li><li>Actual performance information</li><li>Input to Change evaluation and CAB meetings</li></ul>	<ul><li>New or changed Services</li><li>Known errors</li><li>Standard changes for use in RF</li><li>Knowledge and information in the SKMS (including the CMS)</li><li>Change Schedule</li></ul>

Lifecycle Phase (...)	Input from SO to ...	Output from ... to SO
Continual Service Improvement	• Operational performance data and Service records • Proposed problem resolutions and proactive measures • Knowledge and information in the SKMS • Achievements against metrics, KPIs and CSFs • Improvement opportunities logged in the CSI Register	• Results of customer and user satisfaction surveys • Service reports and dashboards • Data required for metrics, KPIs, CSFs • RFCs for implementing improvements

From: *ITIL® Service Operation*, Table 3.5. ©Crown copyright 2011. Reproduced under license from the Cabinet Office.

Event Management (EM)

Purpose

Manage events through their lifecycle (detect, understand, action, closure).

Objectives

- Detect defined changes of state that are significant to the organization.
- Determine appropriate actions for each event type and communicate to appropriate functional groups.
- Define the trigger which initiates SO processes and operational activities.
- Provide data for "actual vs design" comparison.
- Provide data for reporting and improvement activities.

Process (...)	Input from EM to ...	Output from ... to EM
Service Strategy		
Strategy Management for IT Services	• MI measuring achievement (or not) of Strategy • Measurements from tools calibrated to indicate if Strategy is effective	• Mission/vision • Service Strategy • Policies • Generic guidelines (scope)of operation (within defined Strategy)
Service Portfolio Management	• Information for events related to a Service • Standard operating procedures • Escalation procedures • Prioritization	• Overall view of Service (how and why delivered)
Financial Management	• Resources used to manage the EM process • Proposed process budget	• Cost of EM • Provide insight into cost for addressing an issue and not addressing an issue
Demand Management	• Provide actual Service utilization via monitoring • Validate PBAs • Event information as it relates to PBAs	• Monitoring thresholds to prevent demand-related events
Business Relationship Management		
Service Design		
Design Coordination		
Service Catalogue Management		

Process (...)	Input from EM to ...	Output from ... to EM
Service Level Management	• Monitoring activities (Service achievements, proactive prevention of failure, etc.) • Service failure • Service threshold alerts indicating a potential breach of SLA/OLA requirement (proactive expectation management)	• Priority and impact of an event based on SLA targets • SLRs
Availability Management	• Events indicating a potential breach of SLA/OLA requirement • Threshold/exception reports	• Availability thresholds for defining monitoring for events • Operational procedures for recognizing, logging, escalating, and communicating events • Defines event significance and thresholds
Capacity Management	• Events indicating a potential breach of SLA/OLA requirement	• Basis for alarms, alerts, thresholds to be included in monitoring • Event correlation tables, rules, and responses • Operational procedures for recognizing, logging, escalating, and communicating events • Defines event significance and thresholds
IT Service Continuity Management	• Communication of an event	• Thresholds for critical (fragile) components (proactive prevention)
Information Security Management	• Reports on security-based thresholds, events, alerts, and warnings	• Critical business applications and/or business processes for monitoring • Thresholds for critical (fragile) components (proactive prevention) • Security-based thresholds, events, alerts, warnings
Supplier Management		
Service Transition		
Transition Planning and Support		
Change Management	• RFC for assessment (based on monitoring thresholds and defined events) • RFC for process improvements • RFC for event-related change • Events that trigger change actions	

Process (...)	Input from EM to ...	Output from ... to EM
Service Asset and Configuration Management	• Event records • CIs related to an event • CI information to update lifecycle status	• Event records (historical) • New CIs which will be monitored • CI baselines in CMS for comparison of current event
Release and Deployment Management	• Information indicating completion of standard deployments, if configured	
Service Validation and Testing		
Change Evaluation	• Data for Evaluation reports	
Knowledge Management	• Additions to the DIK structure (event-related) of the SKMS	• Relevant, timely, required and accurate knowledge, information, and data
Service Operation		
Incident Management	• Identified Service events and related information, including resolution (e.g. self-healing, etc.) • Escalated event for IM activities	• Incidents related to an event • Communication of resolved incident • Communication that escalated event was not an incident (monitoring correction via ChM)
Request Fulfillment	•	•
Problem Management	• Event triggering PM activities • Information to trigger proactive problem-solving	• Problems related to an event • Communication of resolved problem • Communication that escalated event was not an problem (monitoring correction via ChM)
Access Management	• Access-related events, if capability included in monitoring	• Access-related data for incorporation into monitoring tools
Continual Service Improvement		
7-step Improvement Process	• Monitoring and data capture capabilities • Data capture for analysis as defined • Assist in automation efforts • Identify improvement opportunities • Specific Service improvements based on EM events	• Monitoring procedures • (Re-)define monitoring thresholds • Recommendations for improvement implantation plans

Function (...)	Input from EM to ...	Output from ... to EM
Service Desk		
Technical Management		• Application of monitoring parameters • Definition of monitoring thresholds (with CapM)
Application Management		
IT Operations Management		• Coordination between process activities and

Incident Management (IM)

Purpose

Restore Services as quickly as possible with minimal impact to business operations; manage all incidents through their lifecycle.

Objectives

- Develop and deploy standardized techniques to perform the activities of IM.
- Efficient/effectively communicate incidents to all who need the information (IT and business).
- Professionally resolve and communicate incidents with the goal of improving business perceptions of IT.
- Ensure alignment between IM and business priorities.
- Improve/maintain user satisfaction.

Process (...)	Input from IM to ...	Output from ... to IM
Service Strategy		
Strategy Management for IT Services	• Execution of strategic priorities • MI measuring achievement (or not) of Strategy	• Mission/vision • Service Strategy • Policies • Generic guidelines (scope) of operation (within defined Strategy)
Service Portfolio Management	• Service recommendations from incident patterns • Standard operating procedures • Escalation procedure • Prioritization	• Overall view of Service (how and why delivered)
Financial Management	• Incident details to assist Service unavailability calculations • Incident details for any FM-related incident (i.e. invoicing, accounting, etc.) • Resources used to manage the IM process • Proposed process budget	• Cost of IM
Demand Management	• Demand-related incidents	• Possible mitigation for demand-related incident
Business Relationship Management	• Satisfaction survey results • Prevented incidents (proactive work)	• Customer satisfaction requirements • Customer perception • Complaints/compliments

Process (...)	Input from IM to ...	Output from ... to IM
Service Design		
Design Coordination	• Incidents related to the design of a Service	
Service Catalogue Management	• Incidents related to the use of the Service Catalogue • Incidents related to the information in the Service Catalogue	• Services available to which customers/profiles
Service Level Management	• Recommendations for updates to incident thresholds • Service outages/incidents • IM capabilities as input to OLAs/Service expectations • Potential Service failure information • Escalation information • Restoration information • Survey results (by Service Desk staff) • Complaints/compliments • Service terms (conditions that can be met by IM staff) • Measures of Service achievements (agreed metrics/measures)	• Service Quality Plan • Agreed Service levels/targets • Thresholds for addressing incidents • Prioritization based on OLAs (IT capabilities) and Service criticality (customer and BRM input) • Service level to assist in classifying incidents
Availability Management	• Availability-related incident information • Unavailability information • Availability data • SFA information	• Expectations/thresholds for availability of Services for identification of incidents • Assist with resolution of any availability-related incident • Reduce gaps in Expanded Incident Lifecycle • Diagnostic scripts
Capacity Management	• Capacity-related incident information	• Expectations/thresholds for capacity of Services for identification of incidents • Assistance in resolution of capacity-related incidents • Advice on workarounds • Diagnostic scripts
IT Service Continuity Management	• Parameters/information on major incident (invoke the Continuity Plan) • Incidents that may invoke the Continuity Plan • Incidents caused during/after invocation of the Continuity Plan (effectiveness of Continuity Plan)	• Invocation of the Continuity Plan parameters

Process (...)	Input from IM to ...	Output from ... to IM
Information Security Management	• Security-related incidents • Security incident escalation	• Definition of "security incident" • Manages all security-related incidents
Supplier Management	• Incidents related to a specific supplier • Incident diagnosis/workarounds • Satisfaction survey results	• Supplier-related information in support of incident diagnosis/workarounds • What Services the provider supports/provides for assigning incidents
Service Transition		
Transition Planning and Support	• Incident handling as related to Transition activities (test/live environments)	
Change Management	• Change-related incidents • RFC for incident resolution • RFC for improved process	• Change Schedule • Details of implemented changes (Change Records) • Authorized emergency changes • PSO • Approved emergency changes details
Service Asset and Configuration Management	• Incident record and updates • CMDB errors • CI attribute and relationship updates • Resolution and closure details • CI status updates	• CI identification • CI relationships • User/caller information • CI owners, maintainers, suppliers • CI status/history • CI warranty information • CI location • CI details for classification, matching, prioritization • CI escalation information • Problem/KE information • Workarounds • Scripts • Provides/maintains diagnostic information • Provides historical view of Incidents • CI status/history • CI warranty information • CI location

Process (...)	Input from IM to ...	Output from ... to IM
Release and Deployment Management	• Details of unexpected post-release events • Service acceptance document (Service Desk)	• Release Plan (roll-out Strategy) • Deployment Plan • Diagnostic scripts • Ensure Service acceptance • ELS parameters • Ensure proper training for correct support capabilities • When a change has been fully deployed • Issues associated with testing failures which are tracked as incidents
Service Validation and Testing	• Test incidents (if IM is active in the development/test environment)	• Known issues with a change to be deployed with options for resolving incidents
Change Evaluation	• Data for Evaluation reports (failures of new/changed Service)	
Knowledge Management	• Accurate capture, store, use, and manage process information and data • Capture of SM data • Fully described actions by support analysts	• Knowledge regarding Services for understanding and troubleshooting incidents • Ensures availability/accuracy of information for knowledge transfer in new or revised support procedures • Relevant, timely, required, and accurate knowledge, information, and data
Service Operation		
Event Management	• Incidents related to an event • Communication of resolved incident • Communication that escalated event was not an incident (monitoring correction via ChM)	• Identified Service events and related information, including resolution (e.g. self-healing, etc.) • Escalated event for IM activities
Request Fulfillment	• Incomplete/inaccurate fulfilled requests creating complaints to Service Desk (and subsequent incident ticket)	• Any requests which were not properly fulfilled or issue with fulfillment workflow, process, system

Process (...)	Input from IM to ...	Output from ... to IM
Problem Management	<ul><li>Incidents related to a problem and/or known error</li><li>Request to open a corresponding problem ticket for an incident</li><li>Incidents submitted after a problem is resolved</li><li>Incident details for root cause analysis</li><li>Incident information for trend analysis</li><li>Proposed workarounds</li><li>Reporting on success/failure (use) of workarounds</li><li>Found root cause in process of managing incident</li><li>"Top 10" Incident list for assessment and processing</li><li>Request for assistance on a major incident</li></ul>	<ul><li>Resolved problems to related incidents</li><li>Workarounds for incidents</li><li>Resources, if necessary to supplement resolution of major incident</li><li>Diagnostic scripts</li><li>KEDB</li></ul>
Access Management	<ul><li>Incidents related to an access profile or standard</li></ul>	<ul><li>Access standards and controls</li></ul>
Continual Service Improvement		
7-step Improvement Process	<ul><li>Assist in automation efforts for incident detection</li><li>Define monitoring thresholds for preventative IM</li><li>Collect data around response times, repair times, resolution times, escalation, telephony metrics</li><li>Collect data around types of calls (requests, incidents, etc.)</li><li>Document and act on incident and telephony trends</li><li>Input to improvement prioritization</li><li>Complaints/compliments</li><li>Identify improvement opportunities</li></ul>	<ul><li>Recommendations for improvement implantation plans</li></ul>

Function (...)	Input from IM to ...	Output from ... to IM
Service Desk	• Procedures	• Ownership all incidents • Detect/record, classify, prioritize, initial support, escalation, and closure activities • Communication on incident status • Monitor progress • Track incident within resolution team
Technical Management	• Procedures	• Training design/delivery for support purposes, as designated in the Design phase (Service Desk) • Diagnostic scripts • Participate in incident resolution activities • Define coding systems (categorization) • Second/third line support
Application Management	• Procedures	• Training design/delivery for support purposes, as designated in the Design phase (Service Desk) • Diagnostic scripts • Participate in incident resolution activities • Define coding systems (categorization) • Second/third line support
IT Operations Management	• Process/procedure documentation	• Non-peak hour support

Request Fulfillment (RF)

Purpose

Manage the lifecycle of all Service Requests.

Objectives

- Efficient/effective processing of Requests (e.g. services, information, complaints, comments, applications, etc.).
- Provide a mechanism to streamline Requests (automation).
- Provide a mechanism to effectively communicate information about status of Requests as well as how to use the system.
- Source/deliver components of standard Services.

Process (...)	Input from RF to ...	Output from ... to RF
Service Strategy		
Strategy Management for IT Services	• MI measuring achievement (or not) of Strategy	• Mission/vision • Service Strategy • Policies • Generic guidelines (scope) of operation (within defined Strategy)
Service Portfolio Management	• List of defined, documented and approved Service Requests	
Financial Management	• Resources used to manage the RF process • Proposed process budget • List of standard Services to be costed	• Cost of RF
Demand Management		• Usage of RF system (total number of hits and breakdown by Request)
Business Relationship Management	• Satisfaction survey results • Use of the RF system	• Customer satisfaction requirements • Customer perception
Service Design		
Design Coordination		
Service Catalogue Management	• Information regarding Service Requests to be published by SCatM	• Published Service Requests
Service Level Management	• Performance reports	• Service targets for fulfillment activities
Availability Management	• RF issues related to availability (track via IM)	• Input to RF workflow designs
Capacity Management		

Process (...)	Input from RF to ...	Output from ... to RF
IT Service Continuity Management		
Information Security Management		• ISM policies and requirements related to Service Requests
Supplier Management	• If the process activities are outsourced, details of a SuppM-related Request event	• If outsourced, contract details for RF workflow designs
Service Transition		
Transition Planning and Support		
Change Management	• RFC for process improvements • RFCs for standard change	• Approved standard changes
Service Asset and Configuration Management	• Service Requests • CI updates	• Service Request records (historical) • Process documentation (request models, workflows, etc.)
Release and Deployment Management	• Workflow for standard changes to be validated by RDM	• Automated Deployment mechanisms for specified requests
Service Validation and Testing		• Results of tests around workflow
Change Evaluation		
Knowledge Management	• Accurate capture, store, use, and manage process information and data	• Fulfill information requests • Relevant, timely, required, and accurate knowledge, information, and data
Service Operation		
Event Management		
Incident Management	• Any Requests which were not properly fulfilled or issue with fulfillment workflow, process, system	• Incomplete/inaccurate fulfilled Requests creating complaints to Service Desk (and subsequent incident ticket)
Problem Management	• Request for support when troubleshooting automation or process activities	
Access Management	• Requests for access • Fulfillment of access requests (if combined process) • Workflows for RF	• Information/process/requirements to support access requests • Authorization "lists" to support access requests for a specific Service

Process (...)	Input from RF to ...	Output from ... to RF
Access Management cont.		• Process/workflow steps to manage access request via RF tool (automation)
Continual Service Improvement		
7-step Improvement Process	• Collect data around fulfillment of Requests (response time, fulfillment activities, etc.) • Document and act on Service Request trends • Identify improvement opportunities • Specific Service improvements based on RF events	• Recommendations for improvement implantation plans

Function (...)	Input from RF to ...	Output from ... to RF
Service Desk	• Workflows for Request fulfillment, if not automated	• Request escalation • Communication (status, queries, etc) to requestor
Technical Management	• Escalated Requests (for fulfillment)	• Completed/fulfilled Requests
Application Management	• Escalated Requests (for fulfillment)	• Completed/fulfilled Requests
IT Operations Management		

Problem Management (PM)

Purpose

Manage lifecycle of problems, prevent incidents, or minimize their impact.

Objectives

- Problem (incident) prevention.
- Eliminate repetitive incidents.
- Minimize the non-preventable incident.

Process (...)	Input from PM to ...	Output from ... to PM
Service Strategy		
Strategy Management for IT Services	• MI measuring achievement (or not) of Strategy	• Mission/vision • Service Strategy • Policies • Generic guidelines (scope) of operation (within defined Strategy)
Service Portfolio Management	• Standard operating procedures • Escalation procedures • Prioritization	• Overall view of Service (how and why delivered)
Financial Management	• Problem details for any FM-related problem (i.e. invoicing, accounting, etc.) • Problem resolution options and benefits for comparative costing • Resources used to manage the PM process • Proposed process budget	• Cost of PM • Submit possible FM problem for investigation • Resource for PM team • Costing options to remove known problem prior to raising RFC
Demand Management	• Demand-related problems • Workarounds for demand-related issues	• Demand-related data for problem investigation/actions
Business Relationship Management	• Prevented outages (proactive work)	• Customer satisfaction requirements • Customer perception
Service Design		
Design Coordination		• Problems that relate to the design of a Service
Service Catalogue Management	• Workarounds for known errors in the Service Catalogue	• Problems regarding the Service
Service Level Management	• Reports on problem activities • Potential threats to Service levels • Proactive prevention for achievement of Service targets	• SIPs • Service levels to assist in classifying problems

Process (...)	Input from PM to ...	Output from ... to PM
Service Level Management cont.		• Prioritization based on OLAs (IT capabilities) and Service criticality (customer and BRM input) • Highlights potential problems • Provides resource for Problem Resolution team
Availability Management	• Problem data • Proactive reporting of potential threats to availability • Root cause analysis • Improvement suggestions • SFA information • Shared tools/techniques (CFIA, FTA, SFA, etc.) • Methods to reduce downtime	• Availability Plan • Assist with resolution of any availability-related problem • Shared tools/techniques (CFIA, FTA, SFA, etc.)
Capacity Management	• Capacity-related problem information	• Assistance in resolution of capacity-related problems • Provides resource for Problem Resolution team • Highlights potential capacity problem
IT Service Continuity Management	• Parameters/information on major problem (invoke the Continuity Plan) • High-risk problems that may threaten Service Continuity • Assistance in understanding the "why" of a failed deployment of the Continuity Plan • Assistance in resolving a failed deployment of the Continuity Plan • Proactive PM methods to avoid a potential disaster	• Invocation of the Continuity Plan parameters • Provides resource for Problem Resolution team
Information Security Management	• Cause and possible resolution of security-related events • Security problem details	• Provides resource for Problem Resolution team, as needed
Supplier Management	• Details of a SuppM-related problem • Investigation of SLA/SLR breaches owing to poor supplier performance	• Provides resource for Problem Resolution team • Supplier-related KE information incorporated into organizational knowledgebase

Process (...)	Input from PM to ...	Output from ... to PM
Service Transition		
Transition Planning and Support	• RCA as related to Transition activities (test/live environments)	
Change Management	• Member of the CAB • Problems associated to change • PIR criteria • PIR participation • RFC for process improvements • Latest information concerning RFC priority • RFC for problem resolution (as well as permanently correct KEs)	• Change Schedule • PSO • CAB Agenda • CAB Minutes • Status on changes that resolve problems • History of changes that have been remediated • Approved emergency changes • PIR procedures • Details of implemented changes (for RCA activities) • Approved emergency changes
Service Asset and Configuration Management	• KEs • KEDB links • Workaround information • CI status updates • Problem records and updates	• CI identification • CI relationships • CI owners, maintainers, suppliers • User/customer information • CI details for classification, matching, prioritization • CI escalation information • Problem/KE records • Information for trend analysis • CI status/history • Incident history (for diagnosis purposes) • Provides/maintains diagnostic information • Provides historical view of Problems • Relationships between CIs for Root Cause Analysis
Release and Deployment Management	• Details of all identified post-Release problems	• Evidence to close problem records • Pre-Release known errors • PIR criteria • Development KEs to live/operation KEDB
Service Validation and Testing	• RCA of test errors owing to procedure/protocol or unexpected results	• Test problems (request for formal investigation)

Process (...)	Input from PM to ...	Output from ... to PM
Change Evaluation	• Data for Evaluation reports (Failures of new/changed Service)	
Knowledge Management	• Accurate capture, store, use, and manage process information and data • Scripts to assist data capture by IM staff for resolution or further analysis • KEDB links (via CMDB/CMS)	• Relevant, timely, required, and accurate knowledge, information, and data (SKMS)
Service Operation		
Event Management	• Problems related to an event • Communication of resolved problem • Communication that escalated event was not an problem (monitoring correction via ChM)	• Event triggering PM activities • Information to trigger proactive problem-solving
Incident Management	• Resolved problems to related incidents • Workarounds for incidents • Resources, if necessary to supplement resolution of major incident • Diagnostic scripts • KEDB	• Incidents related to a problem and/or known error • Request to open a corresponding problem ticket for an incident • Incidents submitted after a problem is resolved • Incident details for root cause analysis • Incident information for trend analysis • Proposed workarounds • Reporting on success/failure (use) of workarounds • Found root cause in process of managing incident • "Top 10" Incident list for assessment and processing • Request for assistance on a major incident
Request Fulfillment		• Request for support when troubleshooting automation or process activities
Access Management	• Workarounds for access issues	• AcM resource for problem-solving team, when necessary

Process (...)	Input from PM to ...	Output from ... to PM
Continual Service Improvement		
7-step Improvement Process	• Root cause investigation for trend cause • Recommended improvements • Input to improvement prioritization • Identify improvement opportunities (reactive and proactive activities) • Specific Service improvements based on PM events	• Recommendations for improvement implantation plans

Function (...)	Input from PM to ...	Output from ... to PM
Service Desk	• KEDB • Resources, if necessary to supplement resolution of major incident	• Communication about incident; request to open a parallel-running problem ticket
Technical Management		• Participate in PM activities • Expertise for analysis/RCA activities • Define coding systems (categorization) • Second/third line support
Application Management		• Participate in PM activities • Expertise for analysis/RCA activities • Define coding systems (categorization) • Second/third line support
IT Operations Management		• Participate in PM activities, when needed and as appropriate • Expertise for analysis/RCA activities, as appropriate

Access Management (AcM)

Purpose

Provide the right access, to the right users for the right services (ISM policy execution that was included in the AcM Service Designs).

Objectives

- Manage access as defined by ISM/AM.
- Effectively and efficiently respond to access requests (e.g. change, revocation, reduction, etc.) within stated policy limits.
- Ensure provided rights are not abused.

Process (...)	Input from AcM to ...	Output from ... to AcM
Service Strategy		
Strategy Management for IT Services	• MI measuring achievement (or not) of Strategy	• Mission/vision • Service Strategy • Policies • Generic guidelines (scope) of operation (within defined Strategy)
Service Portfolio Management	• Reports on requests for Service Portfolio access • Reports on unauthorized access attempts	• User access/profile requirements • List of users/groups authorized to access the Service Portfolio
Financial Management	• Resources used to manage the AcM process • Proposed process budget	• Cost of AcM • Cost of access controls
Demand Management	• Access granted per Service	
Business Relationship Management	• Reports on rights granted, rejected • Reports on unauthorized Service access attempts • Reports on Service access breaches	• Projected user community
Service Design		
Design Coordination		• Requests for access to design data, tools, etc. for staff (new and outgoing, etc.)
Service Catalogue Management	• Information (requirements) for getting access to Services	
Service Level Management	• Reports on unauthorized Service access attempts • Reports on Service access breaches	• SLRs/SLAs containing requirements for managing access to the Service
Availability Management	• Reports on rights granted/revoked	• Methods for granting/revoking rights

Process (...)	Input from AcM to ...	Output from ... to AcM
Capacity Management		
IT Service Continuity Management	• Reports of access granted • Access requests for suppliers or external parties • Assurance access controls effective/active in failover environment	• Overall security standards within which AcM must perform • Authorization (with AM) policies for granting data/information/Service access
Information Security Management	• Recommended updates to the overall Security Management Strategy • Reports of access granted/changed/revoked • Access requests for suppliers or external parties • Assurance access controls effective/active in failover environment	• Overall security standards within which AcM must perform • Authorization (with AM) policies for granting data, information, Service access
Supplier Management	• Reports on Supplier access provided (rejected)	• Requirements for third party access to Services, CIs, data, etc.
Service Transition		
Transition Planning and Support		
Change Management	• RFCs for access control modifications • RFC for process improvements	• Approved access control actions
Service Asset and Configuration Management	• Access controls for CIs • Profile/user attribute definitions	• Access control information (ISM/AM)
Release and Deployment Management		
Service Validation and Testing	• Testing of Service access requirements, etc.	• Test results of access control measures
Change Evaluation		
Knowledge Management	• Provide access rights to the SKMS based on ISM/AM policies • General information for organization around access (grant, revoke, reduce, change)	• Relevant, timely, required, and accurate knowledge, information, and data (SKMS)

Process (...)	Input from AcM to ...	Output from ... to AcM
Service Operation		
Event Management	• Access-related data for incorporation into monitoring tools	• Access-related events, if capability included in monitoring
Incident Management	• Access standards and controls	• Incidents related to an access profile or standard
Request Fulfillment	• Information/process/requirements to support access requests • Authorization "lists" to support access requests for a specific Service • Process/workflow steps to manage access request via RF tool (automation)	• Requests for access • Fulfillment of access requests (if combined process) • Workflows for RF
Problem Management	• AcM resource for problem-solving team, when necessary	• Workarounds for access issues
Continual Service Improvement		
7-step Improvement Process	• Identify improvement opportunities • Specific Service improvements based on Access Management events	• Recommendations for improvement implantation plans

Function (...)	Input from AcM to ...	Output from ... to AcM
Service Desk		• If access requests managed at the Service Desk, reports on activities with their purview • Incidents related to access
Technical Management		• Process and procedure to update ACLs • Complete process tasks (add, remove, and modify access)
Application Management		• Complete process tasks (add, remove, and modify access)
IT Operations Management		

Continual Service Improvement (CSI)

Purpose

Improve service/process/cost effectiveness by aligning Services with business needs through defined and implemented improvements.

Objectives

- Analyze, review, and suggest improvements throughout the entire lifecycle.
- Review and analyze Service achievements to identify and implement improvements (cost, quality, efficiency, effectiveness).
- Ensure all improvement initiatives do not negatively impact customer satisfaction.
- Ensure "quality" remains at the forefront of all improvement initiatives.
- Ensure all actions are measurable and that those measure are clearly defined and reviewed for accuracy and relevance.

Lifecycle stage (...)	Inputs from CSI to ...	Outputs from ... to CSI
Service Strategy	<ul><li>Results of customer and user satisfaction surveys</li><li>Input to business cases and the Service Portfolio</li><li>Feedback on strategies and policies</li><li>Financial information regarding improvement initiatives for input to budgets</li><li>Data required for metrics, KPIs and CSFs</li><li>Service reports</li><li>RFCs for implementing improvements</li></ul>	<ul><li>Vision and mission</li><li>Service Portfolio</li><li>Policies</li><li>Strategies and strategic plans</li><li>Priorities</li><li>Financial information and budgets</li><li>PBAs</li><li>Achievements against metrics, KPIs, CSFs</li><li>Improvement opportunities logged in the CSI Register</li></ul>
Service Design	<ul><li>Results of customer and user satisfaction surveys</li><li>Input to design requirements</li><li>Data required for metrics, KPIs and CSFs</li><li>Service reports</li><li>Feedback SDPs</li><li>RFCs for implementing improvements</li></ul>	<ul><li>Service Catalogue</li><li>SDPs including details of utility and warranty</li><li>Knowledge and information in the SKMS</li><li>Achievements against metrics, KPIs and CSFs</li><li>Design of Services, measurements, processes, infrastructure, and systems</li><li>Design for the 7S and procedures</li><li>Improvement opportunities logged in the CSI Register</li></ul>

Lifecycle stage (...)	Inputs from CSI to ...	Outputs from ... to CSI
Service Transition	• Results of customer and user satisfaction surveys • Input to testing requirements • Data required for metrics, KPIs and CSFs • Input to ChE and CAB meetings • Service reports • RFCs for implementing improvements	• Test reports • ChE reports • Knowledge and information in the SKMS • Achievements against metrics, KPIs and CSFs • Improvement opportunities logged in the CSI Register
Service Operation	• Results of customer and user satisfaction surveys • Service reports and dashboards • Data required for metrics, KPIs and CSFs • RFCs for implementing improvements	• Operational performance data and Service records • Proposed problem resolutions and proactive measures • Knowledge and information in the SKMS • Achievements against metrics, KPIs and CSFs • Improvement opportunities logged in the CSI register

From: *ITIL® Continual Service Improvement*, Table 3.1. © Crown copyright 2011. Reproduced under license from the Cabinet Office.

7-step Improvement Process (7S)

Purpose

Define and manage the process activities for improvements (identify, define, gather, process, analyze, present, implement).

Objectives

- Identify tool, Service product, process, and so on, improvements.
- Ensure business outcomes are met in the most cost-effective manner but not to the detriment of Service quality.
- Define improvement opportunities via effective data manipulation and analysis (defined, gathered, measured, analyzed).
- Ensure ongoing business outcome achievement via assessment and review (align and re-align actions to meet business outcomes).
- Clearly define all measurements; document their purpose and interpretation.

Process (...)	Input from 7S to ...	Output from ... to 7S
Service Strategy		
Strategy Management for IT Services	<ul><li>Measurements/reports as to the effective Strategy execution</li><li>Evaluate Strategy for effectiveness</li><li>Improvements to Strategy (process, Service, etc.)</li><li>Gap analysis (as-is vs to-be; planned vs actual, etc.)</li><li>Service improvement opportunities</li><li>Improvement possibilities for assessment against the Strategy</li><li>Recommendations for improvement implantation plans</li></ul>	<ul><li>Mission/vision</li><li>Service Strategy</li><li>Policies</li><li>Strategic parameters</li><li>Service improvement opportunities</li><li>Specific Service improvements based on StM events</li><li>Corporate, divisional and departmental goals/objectives</li><li>Legislative/regulatory requirements</li><li>Governance requirements</li><li>Risk assessment</li><li>Identify improvement opportunities</li></ul>
Service Portfolio Management	<ul><li>Improvement possibilities for assessment against the current Service Portfolio</li><li>Business case evaluation</li><li>Validate Service objectives</li><li>Analysis of actual vs anticipated use and return of various Services (use to improve Services, make changes to the mix or availability of Services)</li><li>Recommendations for improvement implantation plans</li></ul>	<ul><li>Service Portfolio</li><li>Service models</li><li>Risk Assessment</li><li>Market expectations (market space analysis)</li><li>Identify improvement opportunities</li></ul>

Process (...)	Input from 7S to ...	Output from ... to 7S
Financial Management	• Resources used to manage 7S • Approved improvements • CSI Register • Proposed process budget • Improvement possibilities for financial assessment (e.g. ROI/VOI, etc.) • Recommendations for improvement implantation plans	• Cost of 7S • Identify improvement opportunities • Specific Service improvements based on Financial Management events • Financial analysis of possible improvement options • Budget cycle • Budget/accounting requirements • Flexible commercial models • Data collection on expenditures vs budget • Cost models (service, location, customer, etc.) • Provide financial tracking templates for budgeting and expenditure reports
Demand Management	• Communication of improvement initiatives • Recommendations for improvement implantation plans	• Identify improvement opportunities • Specific Service improvements based on demand-related events
Business Relationship Management	• Agreed improvements (pending ChM) • Recommendations for improvement implantation plans	• Confirmation of improvements (business benefit) • Specific Service improvements based on BRM events • Business plans and strategy • Service review meetings • Customer satisfaction surveys • New business requirements • Report format • Customer Portfolio • Customer Agreement Portfolio (SLM) • Complaints/compliments • Identify improvement opportunities
Service Design		
Design Coordination	• Assessed improvements (accepted or rejected) • Service improvement opportunities • Business Case	• Proposed improvements to process and design activities • Specific Service improvements based on DC event(s) • SDP • Ensure monitoring/measuring criteria are included in designs • Ensure CSFs/KPIs are measurable and effective

Process (...)	Input from 7S to ...	Output from ... to 7S
Service Catalogue Management	• Communication of improvement initiatives • Update to Service description • Recommendations for improvement implantation plans	• Service Catalogue • Identify improvement opportunities
Service Level Management	• CSI Register • Process improvement opportunities • Agreed Service improvements • Updated/addressed SIP(s) • Recommendations for improvement implantation plans	• SIP • Service Quality Plan • Specific Service improvements based on SLM events • Service review meetings • Updates SLAM chart, scorecards, etc. • Service Level Targets • Service Level analysis • SLAs, OLAs to meet needs and capabilities • Defines what is measured and reported via negotiations with the business • Ensures all agreed measures (SLAs) are actually measurable • Complaints/compliments • Identify improvement opportunities
Availability Management	• CSI Register • Updated Availability Plan • Recommendations for improvement implantation plans	• Proactive Service/component availability opportunities • Specific Service improvements based on Availability Management events • Risk assessment and mitigation plans • Availability Plan • Assist in defining monitoring and data collection capabilities • Accountable for infrastructure monitoring and data collection • Ensure proper tools are in place for data gathering • Trend information on Service/component use and analysis of data from a historical perspective • Assess component performance against technical specification • Input to improvement prioritization • Identify improvement opportunities
Capacity Management	• Updated Capacity Plan • Monitoring procedures/plan	• Process improvement opportunities

147

Process (...)	Input from 7S to ...	Output from ... to 7S
Capacity Management cont.	• Recommendations for improvement implantation plans	• Specific Service improvements based on CapM event • Risk assessment and mitigation plans • Capacity Plan • Trend analysis • Monitored data • New technology impact • Assist in defining monitoring and data collection capabilities • Accountable for infrastructure monitoring and data collection • Ensure proper tools are in place for data gathering • Trend information on Service/component use and analysis of data from a historical perspective • Assess component performance against technical specification • Input to improvement prioritization • Identify improvement opportunities
IT Service Continuity Management	• Updated ITSCM Plan • Process improvement opportunities • Recommendations for improvement implantation plans	• Risk assessment and mitigation plans • ITSCM Plan • Identify improvement opportunities based on ITSCM events
Information Security Management	• Communication of improvement initiatives • Recommendations for improvement implantation plans	• Specific Service improvements based on ISM events • Risk assessment and mitigation plans • Define monitoring for security based on organizational security policies • Collect data around CIA of data/information • Trend analysis of security breaches • Document/assess security-related incidents for trends and cause • Validate success of risk mitigation efforts • Identify improvement opportunities
Supplier Management	• Process improvement opportunities • CSI register • Communication of improvement initiatives	• UCs • Identify improvement opportunities • Specific Service improvements based on SuppM events

Process (...)	Input from 7S to ...	Output from ... to 7S
Supplier Management cont.	• Recommendations for improvement implantation plans	
Service Transition		
Transition Planning and Support	• Recommendations for improvement implantation plans	• Tests/reports on monitoring procedures and measurement criteria • Finalize monitoring procedures for ongoing operations • Identify improvement opportunities
Change Management	• Improvement RFCs, charters, and proposals • Participate in CAB/PIR meetings, if necessary • Recommendations for improvement implantation plans	• Results of RFC, proposal, charter assessments (approved/rejected) • Change Schedule • Identify improvement opportunities
Service Asset and Configuration Management	• Recommendations for improvement implantation plans	• Benchmark data • Baseline data • Identify improvement opportunities
Release and Deployment Management	• Recommendations for improvement implantation plans	• Deployment of approved improvement • Identify improvement opportunities
Service Validation and Testing	• Process improvement opportunities • Recommendations for improvement implantation plans	• Identify improvement opportunities • Service improvement opportunities (from failed tests)
Change Evaluation	• Recommendations for improvement implantation plans	• Identify improvement opportunities
Knowledge Management	• Updated CSI Register • Accurate capture, store, use of management process information and data • Recommendations for improvement implantation plans	• Relevant, timely, required, and accurate knowledge, information, and data (SKMS) • Process improvement opportunities
Service Operation		
Event Management	• Monitoring procedures • (Re-)define monitoring thresholds • Recommendations for improvement implantation plans	• Monitoring and data capture capabilities • Data capture for analysis as defined • Assist in automation efforts • Identify improvement opportunities • Specific Service improvements based on EM events

Process (...)	Input from 7S to ...	Output from ... to 7S
Incident Management	• Recommendations for improvement implantation plans	• Assist in automation efforts for incident detection • Define monitoring thresholds for preventative IM • Collect data around response times, repair times, resolution times, escalation, telephony metrics • Collect data around types of calls (requests, incidents, etc.) • Document and act on incident and telephony trends • Input to improvement prioritization • Complaints/compliments • Identify improvement opportunities
Request Fulfillment	• Recommendations for improvement implantation plans	• Collect data around fulfillment of requests (response time, fulfillment activities, etc.) • Document and act on Service Request trends • Identify improvement opportunities
Problem Management	• Recommendations for improvement implantation plans	• Root cause investigation for trend cause • Recommended improvements • Input to improvement prioritization • Identify improvement opportunities
Access Management	• Recommendations for improvement implantation plans	• Identify improvement opportunities • Specific Service improvements based on Access Management events
Continual Service Improvement		
7-step Improvement Process	• Updated CSI Register	• Benchmark data • CSI Register • Gap Analysis

Function (...)	Input from 7S to ...	Output from ... to 7S
Service Desk	• CSI Register access (status of improvements or suggested improvements)	• Complaints (use for improvements)
Technical Management		• Technical groups will collect and analyze the data • Technical groups that will perform the necessary tasks to plan, design, build, test, deploy improvements (underpin all processes) • Review/confirm analysis/reports • Identify areas for improvement • Evaluate alternate solutions
Application Management		• Application groups will collect and analyze the data • Application groups that will perform the necessary tasks to plan, design, build, test, deploy improvements (underpin all processes) • Review/confirm analysis/reports
IT Operations Management		

Process Work Products

Definition of Work Products

The following table represents the products (e.g. documents, completed actions, outputs, and so on) from the Service Management processes. Use these tables in the same manner as the relationship tables – consider the product and ask if it will have an impact on your Service Management activities. If so, then formally incorporate it. If not, we would strongly encourage you to review the product if only because of its "best practice" nature. Ensure the concepts from the product are considered for inclusion in your management system.

Process	Work Products
Service Strategy	
Strategy Management	• New/Updated Service Strategy • Supporting tactical plans • Review schedule • Mission/vision statement • Policies (plan Execution, Service Design, Transition, operation, improvement) • Strategy requirements for new/changed Services • Business outcomes met (and how) • Project Portfolio (PMO)
Service Portfolio Management	• Up-to-date Service Portfolio • Service charters for new/changed Services • Status reports on new/changed Services • Investment reports on Services in Portfolio • ROI of Services in Portfolio • Service models • Market spaces • Change proposals for assessment and work scheduling for Service charters • Strategic risks • Service Package • CMS • Application Portfolio • Customer Portfolio • Customer Agreement Portfolio • Project Portfolio • Service models • Market spaces
Financial Management	• Charging policies • Budgets • Service costs • Cost models • Service valuation • Service investment analysis

Process	Work Products
Financial Management cont.	• Compliance • Cost optimization • BIA • Planning confidence • Pricing • Cost of change • ROI/VOI calculations • Incentives/penalties
Demand Management	• UPs • PBAs (in Service and Customer Portfolio) • Policies to manage demand (over-utilization) • Policies to manage utilization that is higher/lower than customer expectation • Differentiated offerings for Service packages
Business Relationship Management	• Stakeholder definitions • Defined business outcomes • Agreement to fund/pay for Services • Customer Portfolio • Service requirements (strategy, design, transition) • Customer satisfaction surveys • Schedules of customer activity • Schedule of training and awareness events • Reports of customer perception
Service Design	
Design Coordination	• Comprehensive/consistent Service Designs • SDPs • Revised enterprise architecture • Revised management system • Revised measure/metrics methods • Revised processes • Updated Service Portfolio • Updated Change Records
Service Catalogue Management	• Documented/agreed definition of "service" • Updates to Service Portfolio • RFC updates • Service Catalogue
Service Level Management	• Customer Agreement Portfolio • Service reports • Service improvement opportunities • SIP • Service Quality Plan • Templates: SLR, SLA, OLA • SLRs, SLAs, OLAs • Reports on OLAs/UCs • Service Review meeting minutes and actions • SLA review and Service scope meeting minutes and actions • Updated Change information • Updated RFCs • Revised UC requirements

Process	Work Products
Availability Management	• AMIS • Availability Plan • Availability/recovery design • Service targets for new/changed Services • Reports on Service availability, reliability, maintainability (vs agreed targets) • Reports on component availability, reliability, maintainability (vs agreed targets) • Risk assessment review and report • Updated Risk Register • Monitoring, management and reporting requirements for Services and components • Test schedules (availability, resilience, recovery) • Planned/preventative maintenance schedules • Input to PSO • Proactive availability measures • Improvements for the SIP • CFIA, FTA, TOP, SFA • Expanded Incident Lifecycle • BIA • AARMSS • MTBF, MTRS, MTBSI
Capacity Management	• CMIS • Capacity Plan • Service performance information/reports • Workload analysis/reports • Capacity/performance reports • Forecasts/predictive reports • Thresholds, alerts, events • Improvements for the SIP • Service details for use in DM • New technologies under consideration
IT Service Continuity Management	• New/revised ITSCM policy/strategy • Recovery criteria • ITSCM Plans • BIA exercise/reports • Risk Assessment (reviews/reports) • ITSCM Testing Schedule • ITSCM test scenarios • ITSCM test reports/reviews

Information Security Management	• Overall ISM policy:
	  o Use/misuse IT assets
	  o Access control
	  o Password
	  o Email
	  o Internet
	  o Anti-virus
	  o Information classification
	  o Document classification
	  o Remote access
	  o Copyright infringement
	  o Asset disposal
	  o Records retention
	  o Supplier access

Process	Work Products
Information Security Management cont.	<ul><li>SMIS (data store)</li><li>Security risk assessment reports/reviews</li><li>Security controls</li><li>Security audits/reports</li><li>Security test schedules/plans</li><li>Security classifications</li><li>Defined Classified information assets</li><li>Reviews/reports on security breaches/major incidents</li><li>Policies/processes/procedures for managing partners/suppliers</li></ul>
Supplier Management	<ul><li>SCMIS</li><li>Supplier/contract performance information/reports</li><li>Supplier/contract review meeting minutes/actions</li><li>Supplier SIPs</li><li>Supplier survey reports</li></ul>
Service Transition	
Transition Planning and Support	<ul><li>Transition Strategy</li><li>Transition budget</li><li>Integrated set of Transition plans:<ul><li>Transition plans</li><li>ChM/SACM plans</li><li>Release Policy, Plan and documents</li><li>Test plans/reports</li><li>Build plans/reports</li><li>Evaluation plans/reports</li><li>Deployment plans/reports</li><li>Transition Closure Report</li><li>Schedule of milestones</li><li>Financial requirements</li><li>Provide Quality Assurance of new/changed Service</li><li>Proactively improve Quality during ST activities</li></ul></li><li>Policies (examples):<ul><li>Service Transition Policy</li><li>All Service Changes through ST</li><li>Adopt common frameworks and standards</li><li>Maximize re-use of established process/systems</li><li>Align ST plans with business needs</li><li>Establish/maintain stakeholder relationships</li><li>Establish effective controls and discipline</li><li>Provide system for KT and decision support</li><li>Plan Release Packages</li><li>Anticipate/manage course corrections</li><li>Proactive management of resources across ST</li></ul></li><li>Ensure ELS, where appropriate</li></ul>
Change Management	<ul><li>Policies</li><li>Remediation Plan</li><li>Rejected/cancelled RFCs</li><li>Authorized changes</li><li>Authorized change proposals</li><li>Service/infrastructure changes</li><li>New/changed CIs</li></ul>

Process	Work Products
Change Management cont.	• Revised Change Schedule • Revised PSO • Authorized Change plans • Change decisions/actions • Change documents/records • Process reports • CAB meeting minutes/actions • PIR meeting minutes/actions • Change Schedule • Change Record (approved/rejected) • Change Window
Service Asset and Configuration Management	• CMS/CMDB(s) • Relationships between CIs • New/updated CI records • Updated asset information • Asset Register • Updated CI information • Snapshots/baselines • Status reports • Audit reports • DML
Release and Deployment Management	• Application Portfolio (typically owned by AppDev) • DML • Release Records • New/changed/retired Services • Release/Deployment Plan • Release/Deployment policies • Service notification • Notification to SCatM on new/updated Service • New tested Service capability and environment • New/changed SM documentation • SLAs, OLAs, UCs • New/changed Service Reports • Tested Continuity Plans • Complete/accurate CI list • Release Package • Service Capacity Plan aligned to business plans • Service Transition Report • ELS plans
Service Validation and Testing	• Testing reports to ChE • Configuration baseline of testing environment • Completed tests (defines outcomes, testing parameters, constraints) • Test results • Analysis of test results • Risks identified in testing • Actual vs predicted risks (after Service in place) • Updated data, information, knowledge for SKMS • Test incidents, problems, KEs

Process	Work Products
Service Validation and Testing cont.	<ul><li>CSI recommendations</li><li>Relationships with third parties, suppliers, etc.</li><li>Policies:<ul><li>SVT policies</li><li>Service Quality Plan</li><li>Risk Policy</li><li>Release Policy</li><li>ST Policy</li><li>ChM Policy</li></ul></li></ul>
Change Evaluation	<ul><li>Interim Evaluation reports (ChM)</li><li>Evaluation Report (ChM)</li><li>Policies:<ul><li>Evaluate Ch before Transition</li><li>ChE identifies risk</li><li>Deviation between predicted and unintended managed</li></ul></li><li>Evaluation Plan</li></ul>
Knowledge Management	<ul><li>SKMS</li><li>Knowledge to make decisions</li><li>KM policies</li></ul>
Service Operation	
Event Management	<ul><li>Communicated and escalated events</li><li>Event logs</li><li>Events classified as incidents</li><li>Events indicating potential SLA/OLA breach</li><li>Events indicating completed tasks</li><li>SKMS inputs</li><li>Reviewed/assessed thresholds</li><li>Reports</li></ul>
Incident Management	<ul><li>Resolved incidents</li><li>Documented actions</li><li>Updated IM records</li><li>Updated incident classification</li><li>New Problem Record</li><li>Reports</li><li>Change-related incidents</li><li>Correctly identified CIs related to incident</li><li>Customer satisfaction</li><li>Input to EM (level/quality of monitoring)</li><li>Communication of incident/resolution</li><li>Escalation</li><li>Workarounds</li></ul>
Request Fulfillment	<ul><li>Authorized/rejected Service Requests (SRs)</li><li>Status reports</li><li>Fulfilled SRs</li><li>Incidents</li><li>RFCs/standard changes</li><li>Asset/CI updates</li><li>Updated Request records</li><li>Closed SRs</li><li>Cancelled SRs</li></ul>

Process	Work Products
Problem Management	• Resolved problems and actions taken • Updated PM records • RFCs • Workarounds • KE records • Reports • Improvement recommendations (process)
Access Management	• Provision of access to Services • Records/history of actions (granted, denied, etc.) • Reports (inappropriate access, abuse of Services) • Access Management standards and guidelines
Continual Service Improvement	
7-step Improvement Process	• CSI Register • Measurement/metric register • Rejected improvements • Authorized improvements (ChM) • Policy updates (SLM, AM, CapM) • Measurement capabilities (e.g. Service levels, satisfaction, business impact, supplier performance, market performance, etc.) • Gap Analysis • Updated AM/CapM plans • Monitoring procedures • Identified tools • Monitoring plan • Data collection • Definition of data integrity • Converted data • Grouped data for easy analysis • Analyzed data • Reports tailored to audience

References

Cabinet Office (2011). ITIL® Continual Service Improvement. London: The Stationary Office.

Cabinet Office (2011). ITIL® Service Design. London: The Stationary Office.

Cabinet Office (2011). ITIL® Service Operation. London: The Stationary Office.

Cabinet Office (2011). ITIL® Service Strategy. London: The Stationary Office.

Cabinet Office (2011). ITIL® Service Transition. London: The Stationary Office.

ISO/IEC (2010). Information Technology – Service Management – Part 4: Process Reference Model (ISO/IEC TR 20000-4:2010). Geneva, Switzerland: ISO/IEC.

ISO/IEC (2010). Information Technology – Service Management – Part 5: Exemplar Implementation Plan for ISO/IEC 20000-1 (ISO/IEC TR 20000-5:2010). Geneva, Switzerland: ISO/IEC.

ISO/IEC (2011). Information Technology – Service Management – Part 1: Service Management System Requirements (ISO/IEC 20000-1:2011). Geneva, Switzerland: ISO/IEC.

ISO/IEC (2012). Information Technology – Service Management – Part 2: Guidance on the Application of Service Management Systems (ISO/IEC 20000-2:2012). Geneva, Switzerland: ISO/IEC.

ISO/IEC (2012). Information Technology – Service Management – Part 3: Guidance on Scope Definition and Applicability of ISO/IEC 20000-1 (ISO/IEC 20000-3:2012). Geneva, Switzerland: ISO/IEC.

ITG Resources

IT Governance Ltd. sources, creates and delivers products and services to meet the real-world, evolving IT governance needs of today's organisations, directors, managers and practitioners.

The ITG website (*www.itgovernance.co.uk*) is the international one-stop-shop for corporate and IT governance information, advice, guidance, books, tools, training and consultancy.

www.itgovernance.co.uk/itsm.aspx is the information page on our website for ITSM resources.

Other Websites

Books and tools published by IT Governance Publishing (ITGP) are available from all business booksellers and are also immediately available from the following websites:

www.itgovernance.eu is our euro-denominated website which ships from Benelux and has a growing range of books in European languages other than English.

www.itgovernanceusa.com is a US$-based website that delivers the full range of IT Governance products to North America, and ships from within the continental US.

www.itgovernanceasia.com provides a selected range of ITGP products specifically for customers in the Indian sub-continent.

www.itgovernance.asia delivers the full range of ITGP publications, serving countries across Asia Pacific. Shipping from Hong Kong, US dollars, Singapore dollars, Hong Kong dollars, New Zealand dollars and Thai baht are all accepted through the website.

Toolkits

ITG's unique range of toolkits includes the IT Governance Framework Toolkit, which contains all the tools and guidance that you will need in order to develop and implement an appropriate IT governance framework for your organisation. For a free paper on how to use the proprietary Calder-Moir IT Governance Framework, and for a free trial version of the toolkit, see *www.itgovernance.co.uk/calder_moir.aspx*.

There is also a wide range of toolkits to simplify implementation of management systems, such as an ISO/IEC 27001 ISMS or an ISO/IEC 22301 BCMS, and these can all be viewed and purchased online at *www.itgovernance.co.uk*.

Training Services

IT Governance offers an extensive portfolio of training courses designed to educate information security, IT governance, risk management and compliance professionals. Our classroom and online training programmes will help you develop the skills required to deliver best practice and compliance to your organisation. They will also enhance your career by providing you with industry standard certifications and increased peer recognition. Our range of courses offers a structured learning path from Foundation to Advanced level in the key topics of information security, IT governance, business continuity and service management.

ISO/IEC 20000 is the first international standard for IT service management and has been developed to reflect the best practice guidance contained within the ITIL framework. Our ISO20000 Foundation and Practitioner training courses are designed to provide delegates with a comprehensive introduction and guide to the implementation of an ISO20000 management system and an industry recognised qualification awarded by APMG International.

We have a unique ITIL Foundation (2 Day) training course designed to provide delegates with the knowledge and skills required to pass the EXIN ITIL Foundation examination at the very first attempt. This classroom course has been specifically designed to ensure delegates acquire the ITIL Foundation certificate in a low-cost, time-efficient way.

Full details of all IT Governance training courses can be found at:
www.itgovernance.co.uk/training.aspx

Professional Services and Consultancy

Our expert ITIL/ISO20000 consultants can help you to understand and manage the relationships between the service management processes and functions, showing how best to create an ITSM environment where processes are properly assessed, managed and continually improved to deliver value.

Using a 'forest' view of the service management processes, we can instil in you a clear understanding of how process output will impact the next process within the lifecycle of a service – and also the probable impact on each of the related processes. In this way, you can ensure that you control and manage so that poor service, unachieved goals and objectives, resource waste and many other risks do not arise in your organisation.

With IT Governance, all stakeholders can embrace the value of service management as described within the ITIL framework.

For more information about IT Governance Consultancy services, see:
www.itgovernance.co.uk/itsm-itil-iso20000-consultancy.aspx

Publishing Services

ITGP is the world's leading IT-GRC publishing imprint that is wholly owned by IT Governance Ltd.

With books and tools covering all IT governance, risk and compliance frameworks, we are the publisher of choice for authors and distributors alike, producing unique and practical publications of the highest quality, in the latest formats available, which readers will find invaluable.

www.itgovernancepublishing.co.uk is the website dedicated to ITGP enabling both current and future authors, distributors, readers and other interested parties, to have easier access to more information. This allows ITGP website visitors to keep up to date with the latest publications and news.

Newsletter

IT governance is one of the hottest topics in business today, not least because it is also the fastest moving.

You can stay up to date with the latest developments across the whole spectrum of IT governance subject matter, including: risk management, information security, ITIL and IT service management, project governance, compliance and so much more, by subscribing to ITG's core publications and topic alert emails.

Simply visit our subscription centre and select your preferences:
www.itgovernance.co.uk/newsletter.aspx